Responsive Web Design with HTML5 and CSS3

Learn responsive design using HTML5 and CSS3
to adapt websites to any browser or screen size

Ben Frain

BIRMINGHAM - MUMBAI

Responsive Web Design with HTML5 and CSS3

First published: April 2012

Production Reference: 1020412

Published by Packt Publishing Ltd.
Livery Place
35 Livery Street
Birmingham B3 2PB, UK.

ISBN 978-1-84969-318-9

www.packtpub.com

Cover Image by J. Blaminsky (jarek@jblaminsky.com)

Credits

Author
Ben Frain

Reviewers
Ed Henderson
Mauvis Ledford
KJAMAN

Acquisition Editor
Robin de Jongh

Lead Technical Editor
Joanna Finchen

Technical Editors
Vrinda Amberkar
Vanjeet D'souza
Sonali Tharwani

Project Coordinator
Kushal Bhardwaj

Proofreader
Aaron Nash

Indexer
Monica Ajmera Mehta

Production Coordinator
Shantanu Zagade

Cover Work
Shantanu Zagade

About the Author

Ben Frain has been a freelance frontend web designer/developer for over a decade, working directly with clients and alongside design agencies worldwide. He also works as a technology journalist, contributing regularly to a number of diverse publications on the Mac platform, future technology, website design and technology systems in the Aviation industry.

Before that, he worked as an underrated (and modest) TV Actor, having graduated from Salford University with a degree in Media and Performance. He has written four equally underrated (his opinion) screenplays and still harbors the (fading) belief he might sell one. Outside of work, he enjoys playing indoor football whilst his body (and wife) still allow it.

Visit him online at www.benfrain.com and follow him on Twitter at twitter.com/benfrain.

Thanks first and foremost to the web community. Without their combined brilliance and generosity in documenting and sharing solutions I wouldn't be able to make things I'm even slightly proud of on the Web.

Next, I'd like to thank the father of responsive web design: Ethan Marcotte. A man I've never met or spoken to but whose methodology now affects the way I build websites on a day-to-day basis. It goes without saying that any imperfections or errors in the way I have presented responsive methodology are entirely mine.

Finally, thanks to my family. Anyone who's watched the (also underrated) Wyatt Earp, already knows, *"Nothing counts so much as blood. The rest are just strangers."*

About the Reviewers

Ed Henderson is an experienced Web Developer with a love for designing and building things online.

Not afraid to get his hands dirty and his feet wet, he is open to most technologies as long as they are useful and fun.

Ed has a degree in Computer Science and runs his own business (Web Man Walking). He has worked freelance, permanent and contracted, and has a vast understanding of all aspects of the industry, from web pages to web apps and social media.

Ed thrives on coming up with fresh ideas. He has been a Programmer, Software Developer, and is now a Web Superhero who likes nothing more than tinkering with all things shiny, fluffy, and fuzzy. Making a difference and turning an idea into a useful, working thing are what floats Ed's boat.

You may not know that Ed is the Dad from Jack Draws Anything, http://jackdrawsanything.com/ and winner of the prestigious .net Social Campaign of the Year 2011 award.

Ed lives in Upper Cockenzie, East Lothian, Scotland with the rest of Team Hendo; his amazing wife, Rose and sidekicks, Jack, Toby, and Noah.

You can follow Ed over at http://edhenderson.com (always a work in progress, so excuse the mess) or on Twitter, @edhenderson.

Mauvis Ledford is a full-stack Web Developer specializing in frontend architecture. He's been working actively in this field for the past 9 years, the last two concentrating on the Mobile Web and HTML5.

He runs his own HTML5 web consultancy, specializing in responsive design and write-once deploy everywhere web applications at http://www.brainswap.me. He has worked or was contracted for Disney Mobile, Skype, Netflix, and many startups in the San Francisco Bay area.

Kamrujaman Shohel has 6 years of experience as a Frontend Engineer and is an expert in multiple areas. He has a strong background as a User Interface/Frontend Engineer, UX Designer, UI Specialist, and Usability Consultant. After graduating in 2004, he started his career as a PHP Developer with SSR IT, before working with Multimode Group (Microsoft Department) as an Analyst. He has always liked frontend development, because he can visually apply his creativity there; this is the reason why he changed his career path in January 2005 to become a successful Frontend Developer. Since then, he has worked with Right Brain Solution Limited, as a Senior Frontend Developer. He has excellent expertise on HTML, HTML5, CSS3, jQuery, jQuery UI, PHP, Photoshop CS5, Photoshop CS5, and Illustrator CS5. For the last two years, he has been working with Trenza Softwares, as a Senior Frontend Engineer (Team Lead), has also been working with Mesovison Consultancy Limited as an IT Consultant, and has been a part-time Freelance Developer. He likes to research interface design, interactivity, user compatibility and comprehensive usability and high end web application functionality. This year, he plans to start writing a book on HTML5, CSS3, jQuery, jQuery Mobile, or jQuery UI. His vision is to establish his own company and a foundation where people will help each other develop their talents.

Unless he is asleep, he is always working. Outside of his work he keeps himself up-to-date by reading technical books and researching frontend engineering. He has excellent knowledge of PHP, C, C#, VB.NET, ASP.NET, CakePHP, Zend Framework, Drupal, Joomla, and WordPress. Though he is a Frontend Engineer, he believes practice makes a man perfect, so he always keeps himself updated with new technologies.

www.PacktPub.com

Support files, eBooks, discount offers and more

You might want to visit www.PacktPub.com for support files and downloads related to your book.

Did you know that Packt offers eBook versions of every book published, with PDF and ePub files available? You can upgrade to the eBook version at www.PacktPub.com and as a print book customer, you are entitled to a discount on the eBook copy. Get in touch with us at service@packtpub.com for more details.

At www.PacktPub.com, you can also read a collection of free technical articles, sign up for a range of free newsletters and receive exclusive discounts and offers on Packt books and eBooks.

http://PacktLib.PacktPub.com

Do you need instant solutions to your IT questions? PacktLib is Packt's online digital book library. Here, you can access, read and search across Packt's entire library of books.

Why Subscribe?

- Fully searchable across every book published by Packt
- Copy and paste, print and bookmark content
- On demand and accessible via web browser

Free Access for Packt account holders

If you have an account with Packt at www.PacktPub.com, you can use this to access PacktLib today and view nine entirely free books. Simply use your login credentials for immediate access.

Table of Contents

Preface

If you think you need to create a "mobile" version of your website—think again!
A responsive web design provides one design that looks great on smart phone,
desktop, and everything in-between. It will effortlessly respond to the size of
the user's screen, providing the best experience possible for both today's and
tomorrow's devices.

This book provides a complete "how-to" of taking an existing fixed width design
and making it responsive. Furthermore, it extends responsive design methodology
by applying the latest and most useful techniques provided by HTML5 and CSS3,
making the design leaner and more maintainable than ever before. It also explains
common best-practice methods of writing and delivering code, images, and files.

If you can understand HTML and CSS, you can build a responsive web design.

What this book covers

Chapter 1, Getting Started with HTML5, CSS3, and Responsive Web Design, defines what
responsive web design is, provides examples of responsive designs, and highlights
the benefits and economies of using HTML5 and CSS3.

Chapter 2, Media Queries: Supporting Differing Viewports, explains what media queries
are, how to write them, and how they can be applied to any design to adapt the CSS
styles for a device's capabilities.

Chapter 3, Embracing Fluid Layouts, explains the benefits of a fluid layout and shows
how to easily convert a current fixed-width design to a fluid layout or use a CSS
framework to rapidly prototype a responsive design.

Chapter 4, HTML5 for Responsive Designs, explores the many benefits of coding
with HTML5 (leaner code, semantic elements, offline caching, and WAI-ARIA
for assistive technologies).

Chapter 5, CSS3: Selectors, Typography, and Color Modes, demonstrates the power of CSS3 selectors, allowing you to target and transform anything with ease. We also use CSS3 `@font-face` rules to create beautiful web typography and explain new CSS3 color modes such as RGB(A) and HSL(A).

Chapter 6, Stunning Aesthetics with CSS3, shows how to create text shadows, box shadows, and gradients with pure CSS3. We also cover how to add multiple background images and create icons with a font.

Chapter 7, CSS3 Transitions, Transformations, and Animations, covers how to create, animate, and transform on-screen elements with nothing more than CSS3.

Chapter 8, Conquer Forms with HTML5 and CSS3, illustrates how to implement cross-browser form techniques that work on everything from the latest smart phones to desktop browsers.

Chapter 9, Solving Cross-browser Responsive Challenges, explains how to make old Internet Explorer versions responsive, adapt a set of links to a menu on mobile devices, serve different content for high-resolution displays, and conditionally load assets with Modernizr.

What you need for this book

You'll need a good familiarity with HTML and CSS. A very basic understanding of JavaScript may also help. A good taste in films will also be beneficial.

Who this book is for

Are you writing two websites—one for mobile and one for larger displays? Or perhaps you've heard of "responsive design" but are unsure how to bring HTML5, CSS3, and responsive design together. If so, this book provides everything you need to take your web pages to the next level—before all your competitors do!

This book is aimed at web designers and web developers who currently build fixed-width websites with HTML 4.01 and CSS 2.1. This book explains how to build responsive websites with HTML5 and CSS3 that adapt to any screen size.

Conventions

In this book, you will find a number of styles of text that distinguish between different kinds of information. Here are some examples of these styles, and an explanation of their meaning.

Code words in text are shown as follows: "HTML5 also accepts a far slacker syntax to be considered "valid". For example, `<sCRipt SrC=js/jquery-1.6.2.js></script>` is just as valid as the prior example."

A block of code is set as follows:

```
<div class="header">
  <div class="navigation">
    <ul class="nav-list">
      <li><a href="#" title="Home">Home</a></li>
      <li><a href="#" title="About">About</a></li>
    </ul>
  </div> <!—end of navigation -->
</div> <!—end of header -->
```

When we wish to draw your attention to a particular part of a code block, the relevant lines or items are set in bold:

```
#wrapper {
  margin-right: auto;
  margin-left: auto;
  width: 96%; /* Holding outermost DIV */
}

#header {
  margin-right: 10px;
  margin-left: 10px;
  width: 97.9166667%; /* 940 ÷ 960 */
}
```

New terms and **important words** are shown in bold. Words that you see on the screen, in menus or dialog boxes for example, appear in the text like this: "For example, the navigation menu doesn't alternate between red and black, the main **THESE SHOULD HAVE WON** button in the content area and the **full info** buttons from the sidebar are missing and the fonts are all a far cry from the ones shown in the graphic file".

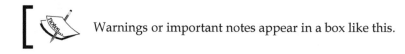 Warnings or important notes appear in a box like this.

 Tips and tricks appear like this.

Reader feedback

Feedback from our readers is always welcome. Let us know what you think about this book—what you liked or may have disliked. Reader feedback is important for us to develop titles that you really get the most out of.

To send us general feedback, simply send an e-mail to feedback@packtpub.com, and mention the book title through the subject of your message.

If there is a topic that you have expertise in and you are interested in either writing or contributing to a book, see our author guide on www.packtpub.com/authors.

Customer support

Now that you are the proud owner of a Packt book, we have a number of things to help you to get the most from your purchase.

Errata

Although we have taken every care to ensure the accuracy of our content, mistakes do happen. If you find a mistake in one of our books—maybe a mistake in the text or the code—we would be grateful if you would report this to us. By doing so, you can save other readers from frustration and help us improve subsequent versions of this book. If you find any errata, please report them by visiting http://www.packtpub.com/support, selecting your book, clicking on the **errata submission form** link, and entering the details of your errata. Once your errata are verified, your submission will be accepted and the errata will be uploaded to our website, or added to any list of existing errata, under the Errata section of that title.

Piracy

Piracy of copyright material on the Internet is an ongoing problem across all media. At Packt, we take the protection of our copyright and licenses very seriously. If you come across any illegal copies of our works, in any form, on the Internet, please provide us with the location address or website name immediately so that we can pursue a remedy.

Please contact us at copyright@packtpub.com with a link to the suspected pirated material.

We appreciate your help in protecting our authors, and our ability to bring you valuable content.

Questions

You can contact us at questions@packtpub.com if you are having a problem with any aspect of the book, and we will do our best to address it.

1
Getting Started with HTML5, CSS3, and Responsive Web Design

Until relatively recently, websites could be built at a fixed width, such as 960 pixels, with the expectation that all end users would get a fairly consistent experience. This fixed width wasn't too wide for laptop screens, and users with large resolution monitors merely had an abundance of margin either side.

But now, there are smart phones. Apple's iPhone ushered in the first truly usable phone browsing experience, and many others have now followed that lead. Unlike the small-screen web browsing implementations of yesterday, that required the thumb dexterity of a Tiddlywinks world champion to use, people are now comfortably using their phones to browse the Web. In addition, there is a growing consumer trend of using small screen devices (tablets and netbooks, for example) in preference to their full screen brethren for content consumption in the home. The indisputable fact is that the number of people using these smaller screen devices to view the Internet is growing at an ever-increasing rate, whilst at the other end of the scale, 27 and 30 inch displays are now also commonplace. There is now a greater difference between the smallest screens browsing the Web and the largest than ever before.

Thankfully, there is a solution to this ever-expanding browser and device landscape. A responsive web design, built with HTML5 and CSS3, allows a website to 'just work' across multiple devices and screens. And the best part is that the techniques are all implemented without the need for server based/backend solutions.

In this chapter we shall:

- Learn the importance of supporting small screen devices
- Define "mobile website" design
- Define "responsive website" design
- Look at great examples of responsive web design
- Learn the difference between viewport and screen sizes
- Install and use viewport changing browser extensions
- Use HTML5 to create cleaner and leaner markup
- Use CSS3 to solve common design challenges

Why smart phones are important (and old IE isn't)

Whilst statistics should only ever be used as a rough guide, it's interesting to note that according to gs.statcounter.com, in the 12 months from July 2010 to July 2011, global mobile browser use had risen from 2.86 to 7.02 percent. The same statistics show that usage of Internet Explorer 6 fell from 8.79 to 3.42 percent. Even Internet Explorer 7 had fallen to 5.45 percent by July 2011. If clients often ask you to "make our site work in Internet Explorer 6 and 7", a fair riposte might be "maybe we should be concentrating our efforts elsewhere?" Far more people are now browsing websites on a mobile phone than with a desktop or laptop running Internet Explorer 6 or 7. That deafening noise you just heard is the collective celebratory whoops of frontend developers around the globe!

So, there are a growing number of people using small screen devices to browse the Internet, and the Internet browsers of these devices have typically been designed to handle existing websites without problems. They do this by shrinking a standard website to fit the viewable area (or **viewport** to give it the correct technical term) of the device. The user then zooms in on the area of content they are interested in. Excellent, so why do we, as frontend designers and developers, need to take any further action?

Well, the more you browse websites, such as the one shown in the preceding screenshot, on iPhones and Android powered handsets, the more apparent the reasons become. It's a tedious and frustrating task to constantly zoom in and out of page areas to see them at a readable size and then move the page left and right to read sentences that are hanging out of the viewport just enough to be annoying, whilst not inadvertently tapping a link you don't want to. Surely we can do better!

Are there times when a responsive design isn't the right choice?

Where budgets allow, and the situation necessitates, a truly "mobile" version of a website could arguably be the preferred option. This could serve up different content, design, and interaction based upon the device, location, connection speed, and host of other variables including the technical capabilities of the device. As a practical example, imagine a pizza chain. It might have one "standard" website and a "mobile" version that adds an augmented reality feature based on your current GPS location to help you find the store. This kind of solution needs more than a responsive design alone can offer.

However, while not every project demands that level of sophistication, in almost all other instances, it would still be preferable to provide users with a tailored view of our content dependent upon the size of their viewport. For example, on most sites, although serving the same content, I'd like to vary the way it's displayed. On small screens, perhaps put elements of less importance beneath the main content, or as a worst-case scenario, hide them altogether. Maybe alter navigation buttons to accommodate finger presses, rather than only offering a usable experience to those able to proffer a precise mouse click! Typography should also be scaled for the sake of readability, allowing text to be read without necessitating constant swipes from side to side. By the same token, whilst catering for smaller viewports, we don't want to compromise the design for those using standard laptop and desktop screens. While we're being all inclusive, what about a few extra enhancements for those with large screens such as 1900 pixels wide and more? In short, I, and I suspect you too, need designs to respond to the entire gamut of viewport sizes that may be used to view them.

Defining responsive web design

The term **responsive web design** was coined by Ethan Marcotte. In his seminal List Apart article (`http://www.alistapart.com/articles/responsive-web-design/`) he consolidated three existing techniques (flexible grid layout, flexible images, and media and media queries) into one unified approach and named it responsive web design. The term is often used to infer the same meaning as a number of other descriptions such as fluid design, elastic layout, rubber layout, liquid design, adaptive layout, cross-device design, and flexible design.

To name just a few! However, as Mr. Marcotte and others have eloquently argued, a truly responsive methodology is actually more than merely altering the layout of a site based upon viewport sizes. Instead, it is to invert our entire current approach to web design. Instead of beginning with a fixed width desktop site design and scaling it down and re-flowing the content for smaller viewports, we should design for the smallest viewport first and then progressively enhance the design and content for larger viewports.

> **Responsive web design in a nutshell**
>
> To attempt to put the philosophy of responsive web design in a nutshell, I would say it's the presentation of content in the most accessible manner for any viewport that accesses it. Conversely, a truly "mobile website" is needed when an experience requires specific content and functionality based upon the device accessing it. In these cases, a mobile website presents an entirely different user experience to its desktop equivalent.

Why stop at responsive design?

A responsive web design will handle the flow of our page content as viewports change but let's go further. HTML5 offers us more than HTML 4 ever could and it's more meaningful semantic elements will form the basis of our markup. CSS3 media queries are an essential ingredient to a responsive design but additional CSS3 modules empower us with previously unseen levels of flexibility. We'll be ditching swathes of background graphics and complicated JavaScript, replacing them with lean CSS3 gradients, shadows, typography, animations and transformations.

Before we get on with creating a responsive HTML5 and CSS3 powered web design, let's first look at some examples of what we should aspire to. Who is already doing a good job with all this new fangled responsive HTML5 and CSS3 malarkey and what can we learn from their pioneering efforts?

Examples of responsive web design

To test your own and others' responsive website designs fully would involve having separate systems set up for every device and screen size. Although nothing betters that practice, the majority of testing can be achieved simply by resizing the browser window. To further aid this method, there are various third-party plugins and browser extensions that display the current browser window or viewport size in pixels. Or in some cases, automatically switch the current window or viewport to a default screen size (1024 x 768 pixels, for example). This allows you to more easily test what happens as screen viewports change.

Attached to pixels? Get over it!

Don't get very attached to pixels as a measurement unit because we will be abandoning them in many instances and moving to relative measurement units (typically, "em" or "ems" and percentages) instead, once we get into responsive web design proper. For reviewing the work of other responsive designs and where those designs change however, they provide a handy reference point.

Get your viewport testing tools here!

Internet Explorer users should make sure that they have the Microsoft Internet Explorer Developer Toolbar. This can be downloaded from the following URL:

`http://www.microsoft.com/download/en/details.aspx?id=18359`

If you are using Safari, my personal favorite is Resize (`http://resizeSafari.com/`), although ResizeMe (`http://web.me.com/aaronholla/Safari_Extensions/ResizeMe.html`) is similar and free.

If you use Firefox, there is Firesizer (`https://addons.mozilla.org/en-US/firefox/addon/firesizer/`) and Chrome users should check out the aptly titled Windows Resizer (`https://chrome.google.com/webstore/detail/kkelicaakdanhinjdeammmilcgefonfh`).

Not a fan of extensions? Here's a further alternative: I wrote a simple HTML page to display the current viewport height and width of a browser window. Using a dab of the JavaScript library, jQuery (`http://jquery.com`), this page gets the current viewport height and width, and displays them. You can keep this page open in another browser tab, resize your window, and then flick back to the website in question to see how it fares. You can find the super simple "What size is my viewport page?" page at the following URL:

`http://benfrain.com/easily-display-the-viewport-size-of-your-page-for-responsive-designs/`

Viewport or screen size?

It's important to understand that viewport and screen size are not the same thing. **Viewport** relates to the content area within the browser window, excluding the toolbars, tabs, and so on. More succinctly, it relates to the area where a website actually displays. **Screen size** refers to the physical display area of a device. Beware that some browser resizer tools display the size, including browser elements such as the URL bar, tabs, and search boxes, and others don't. In the following screenshot, the actual viewport size is shown at the top-right position (**1156 x 921 px**) whilst the Firesizer plugin shows the window size at the bottom-right position (**1171 x 1023**).

Now, we're armed with everything we need to start appreciating the best that the responsive web has to offer. Fire up your browser of choice, engage your screen size tool, and take a look at `http://thinkvitamin.com/`.

If you are viewing the page with a viewport larger than 1060 pixel wide, you will see a layout similar to the one shown in the following screenshot:

If however, you're viewing the site with a viewport larger than 930 pixels but lower than 1060 pixels, you will see a layout, as shown in the following screenshot:

Notice how the main navigation to the side of the logo has changed? The icons to the right of the main content have been arranged to sit one under another. Everything is perfectly usable, and most importantly, isn't disappearing off the screen. Now, take a look with a viewport less than 880 pixels, in the following screenshot:

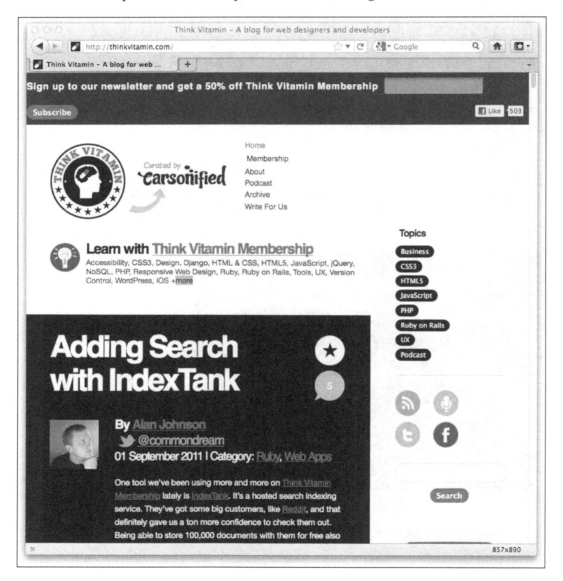

The header remains similar but notice that the right-hand sidebar is thinner still; the icons are now 2 by 2 whilst the text blocks have adjusted and the text is flowing accordingly within the block.

However, reduce your viewport to less than 600 pixel in width and you will notice a major change, as shown in the following screenshot:

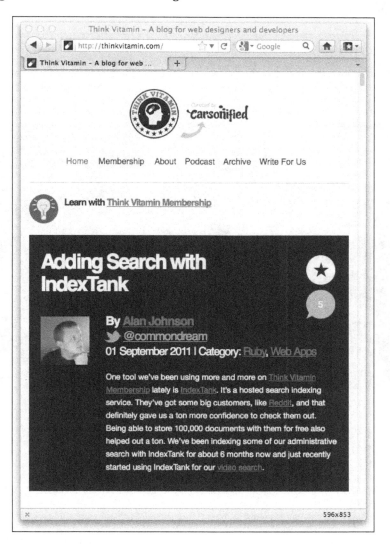

How about that? The entire sidebar has responded to our new viewport, letting the most important part of the site, the content, enjoy the full width of the browser window. Notice also how the header links are now horizontal, as opposed to being at the side of the logo, and the logo itself has resized? All these changes help to create a better experience for the user based upon the viewport dimensions.

Let's look at another example, `http://2011.dconstruct.org/`. With a wide viewport (say, more than 1350 pixels) the site looks like the one shown in the following screenshot:

Notice particularly the grid of nine images. As you decrease the width of the viewport (to less than around 960 pixels), notice what happens? The grid of three rows of three images becomes three rows of two images and one row of three at the bottom, as shown in the following screenshot:

Decreasing the width of our viewport smaller still, at less than around 720 pixels we encounter another design "break point"; the header links switch to include images that provide a better target area for touchscreen navigation:

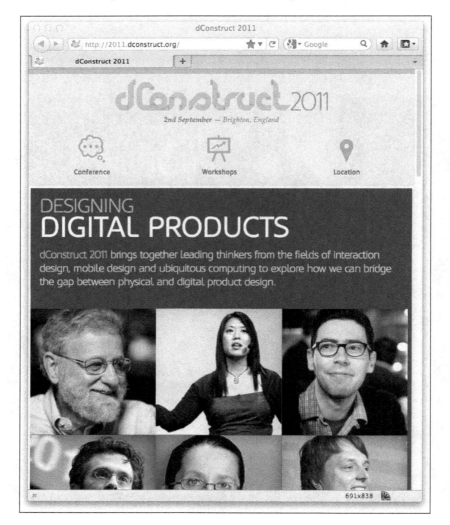

Smaller still, once we reduce the viewport to less than 480 pixels wide, the image grid changes again, now showing a row of two images, then three, and then four. These images continue to resize as the viewport is shrunk to around 300 pixels. To illustrate, the following screenshot shows how it looks on an iPhone:

Online sources of inspiration

One web destination that is useful for inspiration is `http://mediaqueri.es`. However, not all websites displayed there necessarily embrace the full responsive methodology of displaying content around small viewports first, and progressively enhancing for larger viewports. Regardless, at this early point, whilst considering the possibilities of what we can do with responsive web design, there are many great examples to draw ideas from. Although viewing these websites and resizing the viewport illustrates what a responsive web design can do, it doesn't demonstrate what's good about HTML5. The benefits of HTML5 occur "behind the scenes" as it were, so let's now turn our attention there and find out what's so great about HTML5.

HTML5—why it's so good

HTML5 places some emphasis on streamlining the actual markup required to create a page that validates to W3C standards and link all our requisite CSS, JavaScript, and image files. For smart phone users, possibly viewing our pages with limited bandwidth, and a key target for our responsive designs, we want our website to not just respond to their more limited viewport but also load in the fastest possible time. Whilst removing superfluous markup elements represents only a tiny data saving, every little helps!

HTML5 offers further benefits and additional features over the previous iteration of HTML (HTML 4.01). Frontend web developers are likely to be primarily interested in the new semantic elements of HTML5 that provide more meaningful code to search engines. HTML5 also enables feedback to the user on basic site interactivity such as form submissions and so on, often negating the need for more resource heavy JavaScript form processing. Again, that's good news for our responsive design, allowing us to create a leaner and faster-loading code base.

Saving time and code with HTML5

The first line of any HTML document starts with the Doctype (Document Type Declaration). This is the part that, if we are honest, gets added automatically by our code editor of choice or we can paste it from an existing boilerplate (nobody really enters the full HTML 4.01 Doctype out, do they?) Before HTML5, the Doctype for a standard HTML 4.01 page would have looked as follows:

```
<!DOCTYPE HTML PUBLIC "-//W3C//DTD HTML 4.01 Transitional//EN"
"http://www.w3.org/TR/html4/loose.dtd">
```

Now, with HTML5, it's merely as follows:

```
<!DOCTYPE html>
```

Now, as I've already conceded, I don't physically type the Doctype every time I write a page, and I suspect you don't either. So, what's the big deal I hear you cry? Well, what about adding links to JavaScript or CSS in your pages? With existing HTML 4.01, the correct way of linking to a script file would be as follows:

```
<script src="js/jquery-1.6.2.js" type="text/javascript"></script>
```

HTML5 makes this easier:

```
<script src="js/jquery-1.6.2.js"></script>
```

As you can see, the need to specify the type attribute is no longer considered necessary. It's a similar case with linking to CSS files. HTML5 also accepts a far slacker syntax to be considered "valid". For example, `<sCRipt SrC=js/jquery-1.6.2.js></script>` is just as valid as the prior example. We've omitted the quotation marks around the script source as well as using a combination of upper and lower case characters in the tag and attribute names. But HTML5 doesn't care—it will still validate at the W3C HTML5 validator (`http://validator.w3.org/`). This is good news if you are sloppy with your code writing but also, more usefully, if you want to shave every possible surplus character from your markup. There are other specifics when it comes to the writing of code that make life easier. But I'm guessing you're not convinced this is all that exciting. So, let's take a quick peek at the new semantic elements of HTML5.

New, semantically meaningful HTML5 tag elements

When you're structuring an HTML page, it's standard fare to mark up a header and navigation section something like this:

```
<div class="header">
  <div class="navigation">
    <ul class="nav-list">
      <li><a href="#" title="Home">Home</a></li>
      <li><a href="#" title="About">About</a></li>
    </ul>
  </div> <!--end of navigation -->
</div> <!--end of header -->
```

However, take a look at how we do it with HTML5:

```
<header>
  <nav>
    <ul id="nav-list">
      <li><a href="#" title="Home">Home</a></li>
      <li><a href="#" title="About">About</a></li>
    </ul>
  </nav>
</header>
```

How about that? Instead of faceless `<div>` tags for every structural element (albeit with added class names for styling purposes), HTML5 gives us some far more semantically meaningful elements to use instead. Common structural sections within pages such as header and navigation (and many more as we shall soon see) get their own element tags. Our code just became far more "semantic" with the `<nav>` tag telling browsers, "Hey, this section right here is for navigation". Good news for us but perhaps more importantly, good news for search engines, too. They'll now be able to understand our pages better than ever before and rank our content accordingly.

When I write HTML pages, I often do so knowing that they will in turn be passed to the backend crew (you know, those cool kids that deal with PHP, Ruby, .NET, ColdFusion, and so on) before the pages ultimately make it to the WWW. To stay on good terms with the backend folks, I often comment the closing `</div>` tags within the code to enable others (and often myself too) to easily establish where `<div>` elements end. HTML5 negates much of that task. When looking at HTML5 code, a closing element tag of `</header>` for example, instantly tells you what element is closing, without the need to add a comment.

We're just lifting the lid a little here on what semantic goodies HTML5 has for us in the toy box. Before we get carried away, we have one more friend to get acquainted with. If there's one thing this whole new era of web design can't exist without, it's CSS3.

CSS3 enables responsive designs and more

If you've been in the web design trade from the mid-1990s, you'll remember that back then, all designs were table-based and the styling was entwined with content. **Cascading Style Sheets** (**CSS**) were introduced as a way of separating design from the content. It took some time for web designers to step into the bold new world of CSS-based design but sites such as `http://www.csszengarden.com` paved the way, showing just what could be achieved, visually, with a CSS-based design. Since then, CSS has become the standard way of defining the presentational layer of a web page, with CSS 2.1 being the current ratified version of the CSS specification. CSS3 has yet to be fully ratified but that doesn't mean that large portions of it aren't fully usable today. The W3C working group note at `http://www.w3.org/TR/CSS/#css3` is as follows:

CSS Level 3 builds on CSS Level 2 module by module, using the CSS2.1 specification as its core. Each module adds functionality and/or replaces part of the CSS2.1 specification. The CSS Working Group intends that the new CSS modules will not contradict the CSS2.1 specification: only that they will add functionality and refine definitions.

Much of the draft W3C specification reads (by necessity) like legalese. In simplistic terms, what matters to us is that CSS3 is built as a set of 'bolt-on' modules rather than a single consolidated whole. As CSS 2.1 is at the core, none of the techniques you use with CSS 2.1 today are abandoned. Instead, certain, more mature modules (as not all modules are at the same state of readiness) of CSS3 can be actively used today, without waiting for the entire specification to be ratified.

The bottom line—CSS3 won't break anything!

Perhaps the most empowering point of note is that there is no penalty in older browsers for including properties that they do not understand. Older browsers (including Internet Explorer 6, 7, and 8) will happily skip over CSS3 properties that they can't process. This gives us the ability to progressively enhance areas of a design for the better-equipped browsers, whilst ensuring a reasonable fall back for the older ones.

How can CSS3 solve everyday design problems?

Let's consider a common design hurdle we all face on most projects—to create a rounded corner on a screen element, perhaps for a tabbed interface or corner of a boxed element such as a header for example. Using CSS 2.1 this could be achieved by using a **sliding doors** technique (http://www.alistapart.com/articles/slidingdoors/), whereby one background image sits behind another. The HTML could look as simple as this:

```
<a href="#"><span>Box Title</span></a>
```

We add a rounded background to the <a> element by creating two images. The first, called headerLeft.png, would be 15 pixels wide and 40 pixels high and the second, called headerRight.png in this example, would be made wider than we would ever anticipate the header being (280 pixels, here). Each would be one half of the "sliding door". As one element grows (the text within our <span> tags), the background fills the space creating a somewhat future proof rounded corner solution. Here is how the CSS in this example looks:

```
a {
    display: block;
    height: 40px;
    float: left;
    font-size: 1.2em;
    padding-right: 0.8em;
    background: url(images/headerRight.png) no-repeat scroll top right;
```

```
  }
  a span {
    background: url(images/headerLeft.png) no-repeat;
    display: block;
    line-height: 40px;
    padding-left: 0.8em;
  }
```

The following screenshot shows how it looks in Google's Chrome (v16):

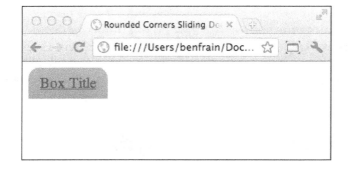

It solves the design problem but requires additional markup (semantically the <span> element has no value) and two additional HTTP requests (for the images) to the server to create the onscreen effect. Now, we could combine the two images into one to create a sprite and then use the background-position: CSS property to shift it around but even with the bandwidth economies that provides, it's still an inflexible solution. What happens if the client decides they want the corners to have a tighter radius? Or a different color? We'd need to re-make our image(s) again. Sadly, until CSS3, this has been the reality of the situation we, as frontend designers and developers have found ourselves in. Ladies and gentleman, I've seen the future, and it's CSS3 shaped! Let's revise the HTML to be only:

```
  <a href="#">Box Title</a>
```

And, to begin with, the CSS can become the following:

```
  a {
    float: left;
    height: 40px;
    line-height: 40px;
    padding-left: 0.8em;
    padding-right: 0.8em;
    border-top-left-radius: 8px;
    border-top-right-radius: 8px;
    background-image: url(images/headerTiny.png);
    background-repeat: repeat-x;
  }
```

The following screenshot shows how the CSS3 version of the button looks in the same browser (Chrome v16):

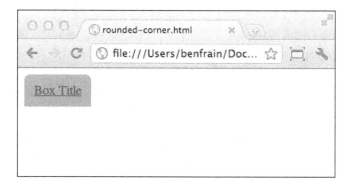

In this example, the two previous images have been substituted for a single 1 pixel-wide image that is repeated along the x-axis. Although the image is only 1 pixel wide, it is 40 pixels high, hopefully higher than any contents that will be inserted. When using an image as a background, it's always necessary to "overshoot" the height, in anticipation of content overflowing, which sadly makes for bigger images and greater bandwidth requirements. Here, however, unlike the entirely image-based solution, CSS3 takes care of the corners for us with the `border-radius` and related properties. Client wants the corners to be a little rounder, say 12 pixels? No problem, just amend the `border-radius` property to `12px` and your work is done. The CSS3 rounded corners property is fast, flexible, and supported in Safari (v3+), Firefox (v1+), Opera (v10.5+), Chrome (v3+), and Internet Explorer 9. Microsoft are so excited about IE 9's support of the feature that (I hope you feel my slight sarcasm seeping through here) they have even designed an interactive page demonstrating the various effects that can be achieved with the `border-radius` property. View this demonstration at the following URL:

`http://ie.microsoft.com/testdrive/html5/borderradius/default.html`

CSS3 can take things further by eliminating the need for a gradient background image by producing the effect in the browser instead. This property isn't as well supported but with something along the lines of `linear-gradient(yellow, blue)`, the background of any element can enjoy a CSS3 generated gradient.

The gradient can be specified in solid colors, traditional HEX values (for example, #BFBFBF) or using one of the CSS3 color modes (more on these in *Chapter 5, CSS3: Selectors, Typography, and Color Modes*). If you're happy for users of older browsers to see a solid background instead of a gradient (as opposed to nothing), a CSS stack something like this would provide a solid color in the event of the browser being unable to handle the gradient:

```
background-color:  #42c264;
background-image:  -webkit-linear-gradient(#4fec50, #42c264);
background-image:  -moz-linear-gradient(#4fec50, #42c264);
background-image:  -o-linear-gradient(#4fec50, #42c264);
background-image:  -ms-linear-gradient(#4fec50, #42c264);
background-image:  -chrome-linear-gradient(#4fec50, #42c264);
background-image:  linear-gradient(#4fec50, #42c264);
```

The linear-gradient property instructs the browser to start with the first color value (#4fec50, in this example) and move to the second color value (#42c264).

You'll notice that in the CSS code, the background-image linear-gradient property has been repeated with a number of prefixes; for example, -webkit-. This allows different browser vendors (for example, -moz- for Mozilla Firefox, -ms- for Microsoft Internet Explorer, and so on) to experiment with their own implementation of the new CSS3 properties before introducing the finished article, at which point the prefixes are unneeded. As stylesheets by their nature cascade, we place the un-prefixed version last, meaning it will supersede the earlier declarations if available.

Look Ma'—no images!

The following screenshot shows how the complete CSS3 button looks in the same browser:

I think you'll agree—any differences between the image version and the entirely CSS version are trivial. Building visual elements with CSS3 allows our responsive design to be far leaner than if we built it with images. Furthermore, image gradients are well supported in modern mobile browsers, the only trade-off being a lack of gradient support for browsers such as IE 9 and lower versions.

What else has CSS3 got to offer?

So far, we've looked at a very mundane example of where CSS3 can help in everyday development tasks. However, let's whet our appetite a little and see what real treats CSS3 allows us. Fire up Safari or Chrome and take a look at `http://www.panic.com/blog/`. Whilst sadly this design isn't responsive, the area of interest for us are the pinned notes at the top. Hover over them and watch as they float out. Nice, eh? In the past this kind of enhancement would have been the domain of resource heavy Flash or JavaScript. Here, it is being achieved entirely through CSS3 transformations. Using CSS3 rather than JavaScript or Flash makes the animation lightweight, maintainable, and therefore perfect for a responsive design. The browsers that support the feature get it, whilst others are none the wiser, merely seeing a static image in its place.

Another great example of CSS3 transformations is `http://demo.marcofolio.net/3d_animation_css3/`. Again, this isn't a responsive web design, we're just looking at the CSS tricks being employed. Take a look at this in Internet Explorer 9 or Firefox first (as of version 9.0, Firefox still didn't support the necessary CSS3 module). Now, take a look in Safari 5+ or Chrome 16+. The following screenshot doesn't do it much justice so if you're not going to take a look you'll have to take my word for it—it's good:

But great looking effects aren't solely the domain of the Webkit-based Safari and Chrome browsers. The following URL works in Firefox too and is another pure CSS3-based solution:

`http://designlovr.com/examples/dynamic_stack_of_index_cards/`

Obviously, these effects are not essential for any website. They are a perfect illustration of "progressive enhancement". In browsers that do not support the effects, they merely see the static images. However, users with more modern browsers can enjoy the visual enhancements. Whilst browser support for CSS3 3D Transformations is rather limited, support for CSS3 rules such as text-shadows, gradients, rounded borders, RGBA color, and multiple background images are all widely supported and provide flexible ways of providing solutions to common design problems that have had us all cursing and scratching our heads for years.

Can HTML5 and CSS3 work for us today?

Any tool or technique should only be used if the application requires it. As frontend developer/designers, our projects typically come with a finite amount of time and resources available to make them financially viable.

As Internet Explorer 7 and 8 don't support the new semantic HTML5 elements or CSS3 properties as standard, if the vast majority of visitors to a site use Internet Explorer 7 or 8, it doesn't make a lot of sense to concentrate your resource on producing a responsive HTML5 and CSS3 based design for it. That doesn't mean doing so is an impossible task. As we shall see in *Chapter 9, Solving Cross-browser Responsive Challenges*, there are a growing number of tools (referred to as **polyfills** as they cover the cracks in older browsers) to patch browsers (mainly Old IE) lacking support for more recent browser features, but adopting a sensible approach to the implementation of a responsive web design from the outset is always the best policy.

In my own experience I typically ask the following from the outset:

- Does the client want to support the largest growing market of Internet users? If yes, responsive methodology is suitable.

- Does the client want the cleanest, fastest, and most maintainable code base? If yes, responsive methodology is suitable.

- Does the client understand that experience can and should be subtly different across different browsers? If yes, responsive methodology is suitable.

- Does the client require the design to look identical across all browsers, including IE 8 and lower versions? If yes, responsive design is not best suited.

- Are 70 percent or more of the current or expected visitors to the site likely to use Internet Explorer 8 or lower versions? If yes, responsive design is not best suited.

It's also important to re-iterate that where the budget allows, there may be times when a fully bespoke "mobile" version of a website is a more relevant option than a responsive design. For the sake of clarification, I term entirely mobile focused solutions that provide different content/experiences to their mobile users as 'mobile websites'. I don't believe anyone advocating responsive web design techniques would argue that a responsive web design would be a suitable substitute for a 'mobile website' in every situation.

Responsive web designs are not magic bullets

At the risk of "teaching Grandma to suck eggs", it's worth re-stating that a responsive HTML5 and CSS3 web design is not a "magic bullet" panacea for all design and content serving challenges. As ever with web design, the specifics of a project (namely budget, target demographic, and purpose) should dictate the implementation. However, in my experience, if the budget is limited and/or the programming of an entirely bespoke "mobile website" isn't a viable option, a responsive web design almost always provides a better and more inclusive user experience than a standard, fixed-width design.

Educating our clients that websites shouldn't look the same in all browsers

The final hurdle to clear before embarking on a responsive design is often one of mindset. And in some ways, this is perhaps the most difficult to overcome. For example, I'm often asked to convert existing graphic designs into standards compliant HTML/CSS and jQuery-based web pages. In my own experience, it's rare (and when I say rare, I mean it's never happened) for graphic designers to have anything other than a fixed-width "desktop version" of a site in mind when producing their design composites. My remit is then to create a pixel perfect rendition of that design in every known browser. Failing or succeeding in this task defines success in the eyes of my client, the graphic designer. This mindset is especially entrenched in clients with a background in printed media design. It's easy to understand their reasoning; a composite of the design can be signed-off by their own clients, they hand it to the frontend designer/developer (you or I), and we then spend our time ensuring the finished code looks as close as humanly possible to that design in all the major browsers. What the client sees is what the client gets.

However, if you've ever tried to get a modern web design looking the same in Internet Explorer 6 and 7 as it does in a modern standards compliant browser such as Safari, Firefox, or Chrome, you will understand the inherent difficulties. It's often taken me as much as 30 percent of a project's allocated time/budget to fix the inherent flaws and failings in these older ailing browsers. That time could have been spent building on enhancements and economizing code for the growing number of users viewing sites in modern browsers, rather than patching and hacking the code base to provide rounded corners, transparent images, correctly aligned form elements, and so on for a shrinking number of Internet Explorer users.

Unfortunately, the only antidote to this scenario is education. The client needs an explanation as to why a responsive design would be worthwhile, what it entails, and why the finished design won't and shouldn't look the same across all viewports and browsers. Some clients get there, some don't. Unfortunately, some still want all the rounded corners and drop shadows to look identical in Internet Explorer 6 too!

When I approach a new project, whether a responsive design is applicable or not, I try and explain the following points to my client:

- By allowing older browsers to display the pages slightly differently, it means that code is more maintainable and cheaper to update in the future.

- Making all elements look the same, even on older browsers (for example, Internet Explorer 8 and lower versions) adds a significant amount of images to a website. This makes it slower, more expensive to produce and more difficult to maintain.

- Leaner code that modern browsers understand equates to a faster website. A faster website ranks higher in search engines than a slow one.

- The number of users with older browsers is shrinking, the number of users with modern browsers is growing — let's support them!

- Most importantly, by supporting modern browsers, you can enjoy a responsive web design that responds to the differing viewports of browsers on different devices.

Summary

We've now established what we mean by a "responsive" design and examined great examples of responsive designs in the wild that make use of the tools and techniques we are about to cover. We've also acknowledged that we need to make a switch from a desktop-centric design mindset and move to a more device agnostic stance, planning our content around the smallest likely viewing area first and progressively enhancing the experience from there. Having taken a glimpse at the new HTML5 specification we've established that there are great portions of it we can use to our advantage today. Namely, the new semantic markup that will allow us to create pages with less code and more meaning than would have been possible previously.

The lynch pin in making a fully responsive web design is CSS3. Before we use CSS3 to add visual flair such as the gradients, rounded corners, text shadows, animations and transforms to our design, we will first use it to serve a more fundamental role. By using CSS3 media queries, we will be able to target specific CSS rules at specific viewports. The next chapter is where we will start our "responsive web design" quest in earnest.

2
Media Queries: Supporting Differing Viewports

As we noted in the last chapter, CSS3 consists of a number of bolt-on modules. **Media queries** is just one of these CSS3 modules. Media queries allow us to target specific CSS styles depending upon the display capabilities of a device. For example, with just a few lines of CSS we can change the way content displays based upon things such as viewport width, screen aspect ratio, orientation (landscape or portrait), and so on.

In this chapter, we shall:

- Learn why media queries are needed for a responsive web design
- Learn how a CSS3 media query is constructed
- Understand what device features we can test for
- Write our first CSS3 media query
- Target CSS style rules to specific viewports
- Learn how to make media queries work on iOS and Android devices

You can use media queries today

Media queries are already widely used and enjoy a broad level of browser support (Firefox 3.6+, Safari 4+, Chrome 4+, Opera 9.5+, iOS Safari 3.2+, Opera Mobile 10+, Android 2.1+, and Internet Explorer 9+). Furthermore, there are easy to implement (albeit JavaScript based) **fixes** for common aged browsers such as Internet Explorer versions 6, 7, and 8. If you need to grab the fixes for Internet Explorer versions 6, 7, and 8 now, you'll need to look at *Chapter 9, Solving Cross-browser Responsive Challenges*. In short, there's no good reason why we can't get using media queries today!

Specifications at the W3C go through a ratification process (if you have a spare day, knock yourself out with the official explanation of the process at `http://www.w3.org/2005/10/Process-20051014/tr`), from **Working Draft (WD)**, to **Candidate Recommendation (CR)**, to **Proposed Recommendation (PR)** before finally arriving, many years later, at **W3C Recommendation (REC)**. So modules at a greater maturity level than others are generally safer to use. For example, CSS Transforms Module Level 3 (`http://www.w3.org/TR/css3-3d-transforms/`) has been at WD status since March 2009 and browser support for it is far scanter than CR modules such as media queries.

Why responsive designs need media queries?

Without the CSS3 media query module, we would be unable to target particular CSS styles at particular device capabilities, such as the viewport width. If you head over to the W3C specification of the CSS3 media query module (`http://www.w3.org/TR/css3-mediaqueries/`), you'll see that this is their official introduction to what media queries are all about:

> *HTML 4 and CSS2 currently support media-dependent style sheets tailored for different media types. For example, a document may use sans-serif fonts when displayed on a screen and serif fonts when printed. 'screen' and 'print' are two media types that have been defined. Media queries extend the functionality of media types by allowing more precise labeling of style sheets.*

> *A media query consists of a media type and zero or more expressions that check for the conditions of particular media features. Among the media features that can be used in media queries are 'width', 'height', and 'color'. By using media queries, presentations can be tailored to a specific range of output devices without changing the content itself.*

Media query syntax

So what does a CSS media query look like and more importantly, how does it work?

Enter the following code at the bottom of any CSS file and preview the related web page:

```css
body {
  background-color: grey;
}
@media screen and (max-width: 960px) {
  body {
    background-color: red;
  }
}
@media screen and (max-width: 768px) {
  body {
    background-color: orange;
  }
}
@media screen and (max-width: 550px) {
  body {
    background-color: yellow;
  }
}
@media screen and (max-width: 320px) {
  body {
    background-color: green;
  }
}
```

Now, preview the file in a modern browser (at least IE 9 if you use IE) and resize the browser window. The background color of the page will vary depending upon the current viewport size. I've used named colors here for clarity but ordinarily you'd use a HEX code; for example, #ffffff.

Now, let's go ahead and break down these media queries to understand how we can make best use of them.

If you are used to working with CSS2 stylesheets you'll know it's possible to specify the type of device (for example, screen or print) applicable to a stylesheet with the media attribute of the <link> tag. You could do so by placing a link as done in the following code snippet within the <head> tags of your HTML:

```html
<link rel="stylesheet" type="text/css" media="screen" href="screen-styles.css">
```

What media queries principally provide is the ability to target styles based upon the *capability* or *features* of a device, rather than merely the *type* of device. Think of it as a question to the browser. If the browser's answer is "true", the enclosed styles are applied. If the answer is "false", they are not. Rather than just asking the browser "Are you a screen?"—as much as we could effectively ask with just CSS2—media queries ask a little more. Instead, a media query might ask, "Are you a screen and are you in portrait orientation?" Let's look at that as an example:

```
<link rel="stylesheet" media="screen and (orientation: portrait)"
href="portrait-screen.css" />
```

First, the media query expression asks the type (are you a screen?), and then the feature (is your screen in portrait orientation?). The `portrait-screen.css` stylesheet will be loaded for any screen device with a portrait screen orientation and ignored for any others. It's possible to reverse the logic of any media query expression by adding `not` to the beginning of the media query. For example, the following code would negate the result in our prior example, loading the file for anything that wasn't a screen with a portrait orientation:

```
<link rel="stylesheet" media="not screen and (orientation: portrait)"
href="portrait-screen.css" />
```

It's also possible to string multiple expressions together. For example, let's extend our first media query example and also limit the file to devices that have a viewport greater than 800 pixels.

```
<link rel="stylesheet" media="screen and (orientation: portrait) and
(min-width: 800px)" href="800wide-portrait-screen.css" />
```

Further still, we could have a list of media queries. If any of the listed queries are true, the file will be loaded. If none are true, it won't. Here is an example:

```
<link rel="stylesheet" media="screen and (orientation: portrait) and
(min-width: 800px), projection" href="800wide-portrait-screen.css" />
```

There are two points to note here. Firstly, a comma separates each media query. Secondly, you'll notice that after `projection`, there is no trailing `and` or feature/ value combination in parentheses. That's because in the absence of these values, the media query is applied to all media types. In our example, the styles will apply to all projectors.

Just like existing CSS rules, media queries can conditionally load styles in a variety of ways. So far, we have included them as links to CSS files that we would place within the `<head></head>` section of our HTML. However, we can also use media queries within CSS stylesheets themselves. For example, if we add the following code into a stylesheet, it will make all `h1` elements green, providing the device has a screen width of 400 pixels or less:

```
@media screen and (max-device-width: 400px) {
  h1 { color: green }
}
```

We can also use the `@import` feature of CSS to conditionally load stylesheets into our existing stylesheet. For example, the following code would import the stylesheet called `phone.css`, providing the device was screen based and had a maximum viewport of 360 pixels:

```
@import url("phone.css") screen and (max-width:360px);
```

Remember that using the `@import` feature of CSS, adds to HTTP requests (which impacts load speed); so use this method sparingly.

What can media queries test for?

When building responsive designs, the media queries that get used most often relate to a device's viewport width (`width`) and the width of the device's screen (`device-width`). In my own experience, I have found little call for the other capabilities we can test for. However, just in case the need arises, here is a list of all capabilities that media queries can test for. Hopefully, some will pique your interest:

- `width`: The viewport width.
- `height`: The viewport height.
- `device-width`: The rendering surface's width (for our purposes, this is typically the screen width of a device).
- `device-height`: The rendering surface's height (for our purposes, this is typically the screen height of a device).
- `orientation`: This capability checks whether a device is portrait or landscape in orientation.
- `aspect-ratio`: The ratio of width to height based upon the viewport width and height. A 16:9 widescreen display can be written as `aspect-ratio: 16/9`.

- device-aspect-ratio: This capability is similar to aspect-ratio but is based upon the width and height of the device rendering surface, rather than viewport.

- color: The number of bits per color component. For example, min-color: 16 will check that the device has 16-bit color.

- color-index: The number of entries in the color lookup table of the device. Values must be numbers and cannot be negative.

- monochrome: This capability tests how many bits per pixel are in a monochrome frame buffer. The value would be a number (integer), for example monochrome: 2, and cannot be negative.

- resolution: This capability can be used to test screen or print resolution; for example, min-resolution: 300dpi. It can also accept measurements in dots per centimetre; for example, min-resolution: 118dpcm.

- scan: This can be either progressive or interlace features largely particular to TVs. For example, a 720p HD TV (the *p* part of 720p indicates "progressive") could be targeted with scan: progressive whilst a 1080i HD TV (the *i* part of 1080i indicates "interlaced") could be targeted with scan: interlace.

- grid: This capability indicates whether or not the device is grid or bitmap based.

All the above features, with the exception of scan and grid, can be prefixed with min or max to create ranges. For example, consider the following code snippet:

```
@import url("phone.css") screen and (min-width:200px) and (max-width:360px);
```

Here, a minimum (min) and maximum (max) have been applied to width to set a range. The phone.css file will only be imported for screen devices with a minimum viewport width of 200 pixels and a maximum viewport width of 360 pixels.

Using media queries to alter our design

As you're, no doubt, aware that CSS stands for Cascading Style Sheet. By their very nature styles further down a cascading stylesheet override equivalent styles higher up (unless styles higher up are more specific). We can therefore set base styles at the beginning of a stylesheet, applicable to all versions of our design, and then override relevant sections with media queries further on in the document. For example, set navigation links as simple text links for the large viewport version of a design (where it's more likely that users will be using a mouse) and then overwrite those styles with a media query to give us a larger target area (for finger presses) for more limited viewports.

The best way to load media queries for responsive designs

Although modern browsers are smart enough to ignore media query targeted files that are not intended for them, it doesn't always stop them actually downloading the files. There is therefore little advantage (apart from personal preference and/or compartmentalization of code) in separating different media query styles into separate files. Using separate files increases the number of HTTP requests needed to render a page, which in turn makes the page slower to load.

The fastest JavaScript tool, Respond.js (`https://github.com/scottjehl/Respond`) for adding partial media query support to Internet Explorer 8 and lower versions is also currently unable to parse CSS referenced by the `@import` command. I'd therefore recommend adding media queries styles within an existing stylesheet. For example, in the existing stylesheet, simply add the media query using the following syntax:

```
@media screen and (max-width: 768px) { YOUR STYLES }
```

Our first responsive design

I don't know about you but I'm itching to get started with a responsive web design! Now we understand the principles of media queries, let's test drive them and see how they work in practice. And I have just the project we can test them on. Indulge me a brief digression…

I like films. However, I commonly find myself disagreeing with others (perhaps that is a contributing factor of me spending my days writing code… alone!), specifically about what is and what isn't a good film. When the Oscar nominees are announced I often have a strong feeling of revulsion in the pit of my stomach. I can't help feeling that different films should be picking up the accolades. I'd like to launch a small site called *And the winner isn't…*, which you'll be able to view online at http://www.andthewinerisnt.com/ on the Web. It will celebrate the films that should have won, berate the ones that did (and shouldn't have) and have video clips, quotes, images, and quizzes thrown in to illustrate I'm correct (I know, I shouldn't need to but I'm good like that).

Don't panic but our design is fixed-width

Much like the graphic designers whom I previously scolded for not considering differing viewports, I started a graphical mockup based around a fixed, 960 pixel-wide grid. In reality, although theoretically it would always be best to start a design thinking about the mobile/small screen experience and building up from there, it's going to be some years until everyone understands the benefits of that thinking. Until then, it's likely you'll need to take existing desktop designs and "retro-fit" them to work responsively. As this is the scenario we are likely to find ourselves in for the foreseeable future, we will begin our process with a fixed-width design of our own. The following screenshot shows what the unfinished fixed-width mockup looks like:

Breaking it down, it has a very simple and common structure—header, navigation, sidebar, content, and footer. Hopefully, this is typical of the kind of structure you're asked to build week in and week out.

In *Chapter 4, HTML5 for Responsive Designs*, I'll tell you why you should be using HTML5 for your markup. However, I'm going to let this slide for now, as we're so eager to test our new media queries skills. So, let's take our first stab at using media queries using good ol' HTML 4 markup. Without the actual content, the basic structure in HTML 4 markup looks like the following code:

```
<!DOCTYPE html PUBLIC "-//W3C//DTD XHTML 1.0 Transitional//EN"
"http://www.w3.org/TR/xhtml1/DTD/xhtml1-transitional.dtd">
<html xmlns="http://www.w3.org/1999/xhtml">
<head>
<meta http-equiv="Content-Type" content="text/html; charset=UTF-8" />
<title>And the winner isn't</title>
<link href="css/main.css" rel="stylesheet" type="text/css" />
</head>

<body>

<div id="wrapper">
  <!-- the header and navigation -->
  <div id="header">
    <div id="navigation">
      <ul>
        <li><a href="#">navigation1</a></li>
        <li><a href="#">navigation2</a></li>
      </ul>
    </div>
  </div>
  <!-- the sidebar -->
  <div id="sidebar">
    <p>here is the sidebar</p>
  </div>
  <!-- the content -->
  <div id="content">
    <p>here is the content</p>
  </div>
  <!-- the footer -->
  <div id="footer">
    <p>Here is the footer</p>
  </div>

</div>
</body>
</html>
```

Looking at the design file in Photoshop, we can see that the header and footer are 940 pixels wide (with 10-pixels margin on either side), and the sidebar and content occupy 220 and 700 pixels, respectively, with a 10-pixel margin on either side of each.

First off, let's set up our structural blocks (header, navigation, sidebar, content, and footer) in the CSS. After inserting the "reset" styles, our super exciting (not!) CSS for the page looks as follows:

```css
#wrapper {
  margin-right: auto;
  margin-left: auto;
  width: 960px;
}

#header {
  margin-right: 10px;
  margin-left: 10px;
  width: 940px;
  background-color: #779307;
}

#navigation ul li {
  display: inline-block;
```

```
}

#sidebar {
  margin-right: 10px;
  margin-left: 10px;
  float: left;
  background-color: #fe9c00;
  width: 220px;
}

#content {
  margin-right: 10px;
  float: right;
  margin-left: 10px;
  width: 700px;
  background-color: #dedede;
}

#footer {
  margin-right: 10px;
  margin-left: 10px;
  clear: both;
  background-color: #663300;
  width: 940px;
}
```

To illustrate how the structure works, besides adding the additional content (*sans* images) I've also added a background color to each structural section.

Just in case you missed the memo, "reset" styles are a bunch of cover-all CSS declarations that reset the various default styles that different browsers render HTML elements with. They are added to the beginning of the main stylesheet in an attempt to reset each browser's own styles to a level playing field so that styles added afterwards in the stylesheet have the same effect across different browsers. There is no "perfect" set of reset styles and most developers have their own variation on the theme. The reset styles I use in HTML 4 documents are a combination of Eric Meyer's original (http://meyerweb.com/eric/tools/css/reset/) and a bunch of personal preferences and tricks I have picked up from studying the code of other incredibly clever folks such as Dan Cederholm (http://simplebits.com). If you don't currently use reset styles, inserting Eric's reset styles at the start of your HTML 4 document will be a good first step. I feel there are better starting points for HTML5 documents, such as normalize.css (http://necolas.github.com/normalize.css/) and we'll look at that in *Chapter 4, HTML5 for Responsive Designs*.

In a browser with a viewport larger than 960 pixels, the following screenshot shows how the basic structure looks:

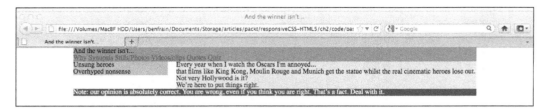

There are numerous other ways the same kind of fixed left/right content structure could be achieved with CSS; you'll no doubt have your own preference. What's universally true of them all however is that as the viewport decreases to less than 960 pixels, areas of the content at the right start getting clipped.

Responsive designs—making images as economical as possible

For the sake of illustrating the problems with the code structure as it is, I've gone ahead and added some of the aesthetic styling from our graphic file into the CSS. As this will ultimately be a responsive design, I've been sure to slice up the background images in the most economical way. For example, for the bunting flags at the top and bottom of the design, instead of creating one long strip as a graphic file, I have sliced around two flags. This slice will then be repeated horizontally as a background image across the viewport to give the illusion of one long strip (no matter how wide things get). In real terms, this makes a difference of 16 KB (the full 960 pixels wide strip was a 20 KB .png file whilst the slice was only 4 KB) on each strip. A mobile user viewing the site over a phone network will appreciate that economy! The following screenshot shows what the slice looks like (zoomed to 600 percent) before export:

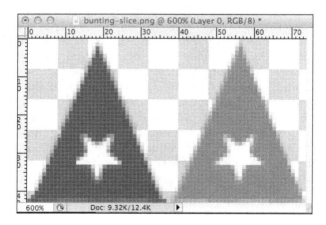

With the background images in place and basic font sizes in place, here is how the *And the winner isn't…* site looks in a browser window:

Style wise, there is still a lot of work to do. For example, the navigation menu doesn't alternate between red and black, the main **THESE SHOULD HAVE WON** button in the content area and the **full info** buttons from the sidebar are missing and the fonts are all a far cry from the ones shown in the graphic file. However, all these things are fixable with HTML5 and CSS3. Using HTML5 and CSS3 to solve these problems, rather than merely inserting image files (as we may have done previously), will make a website in tune with our responsive goal. Remember that we want our code and data overheads as lean as possible to afford users with limited bandwidth speeds an enjoyable experience.

Content clipping in smaller viewports

For now, let's put aside the aesthetic problems and keep focused on the fact than when the viewport is reduced below 960 pixels, there is some seriously nasty clipping on our work in progress home page:

We've only reduced it to 673 pixels wide; imagine how bad it must look on something like an iPhone 3GS? That only has a 320 x 480 pixel display. Just take a look at the following screenshot:

Oh, hang on, this is embarrassing, as it looks just fine, well kind of... Of course, the iOS Safari browser automatically draws pages onto a 980 pixel wide canvas and then squeezes that canvas down to fit the viewport area. We still have to zoom in to see areas but there's no content being clipped. How do we stop Safari and other mobile browsers from doing this?

Stopping modern mobile browsers from auto-resizing the page

Both iOS and Android browsers are based on WebKit (http://www.webkit.org/). These browsers, and a growing number of others (Opera Mobile, for example), allow the use of a specific meta viewport element to override that default canvas shrinking trick. The <meta> tag is simply added within the <head> tags of the HTML. It can be set to a specific width (which we could specify in pixels, for example) or as a scale, for example 2.0 (twice the actual size). Here's an example of the viewport meta tag set to show the browser at twice (200 percent) the actual size:

```
<meta name="viewport"  content="initial-scale=2.0,width=device-width"
/>
```

Let's stick that into our HTML as done in the following code snippet:

```
<!DOCTYPE html PUBLIC "-//W3C//DTD XHTML 1.0 Transitional//EN"
"http://www.w3.org/TR/xhtml1/DTD/xhtml1-transitional.dtd">
<html xmlns="http://www.w3.org/1999/xhtml">
<head>
<meta http-equiv="Content-Type" content="text/html; charset=UTF-8" />
<meta name="viewport" content="initial-scale=2.0,width=device-width"
/>
<title>And the winner isn't…</title>
```

Now, we'll load that page up in Android and see how it looks:

As you can see, this isn't exactly what we're gunning for but it illustrates the point, in a big way!

> **Getting the iOS and Android emulators**
>
> Although there is no substitute for testing sites on real devices, there are emulators for Android and iOS. Android emulator for Windows, Linux and Mac is available free by downloading and installing the Android Software Development Kit (SDK) at `http://developer.android.com/sdk/`. It's a command line setup; so not for the faint hearted. The iOS simulator is only available to Mac OS X users and comes as part of the Xcode package (free from the Mac App Store). Once Xcode is installed, you can access it from `~/Developer/Platforms/ iPhoneSimulator.platform/Developer/Applications iOS Simulator.app`.

Let's break the above `<meta>` tag down and understand what's going on. The `name="viewport"` attribute is obvious enough. The `content="initial-scale=2.0` section is then saying, *scale the content to twice the size* (where 0.5 would be half the size, 3.0 would be three times the size and so on) whilst the `width=device-width` part tells the browser that the width of the page should be equal to `device-width`.

The `<meta>` tag can also be used to control the amount a user can zoom in and out of the page. This example allows users to go as large as three times the device width and as small as half the device width:

```
<meta name="viewport" content="width=device-width, maximum-scale=3,
minimum-scale=0.5" />
```

You could also disable users from zooming at all, although as zooming is an important accessibility tool, it's rare that it would be appropriate in practice:

```
<meta name="viewport" content="initial-scale=1.0, user-scalable=no" />
```

The `user-scalable=no` being the relevant part.

Right, we'll change the scale to 1.0, which means that the mobile browser will render the page at 100 percent of its viewport. Setting it to the device's width means that our page should render at 100 percent of the width of all supported mobile browsers. Here's the `<meta>` tag we'll be using:

```
<meta name="viewport" content="width=device-width,initial-scale=1.0"
/>
```

Looking at our page on an iPad in portrait mode now shows the content being clipped but not as if we are looking through a pair of jam-jar spectacles! This is how we want it at this point. This is progress, trust me!

Noticing that the viewport meta element is seeing increasing use, the W3C is making attempts to bring the same capability into CSS. Head over to `http://dev.w3.org/csswg/css-device-adapt/` and read all about the new `@viewport` declaration. The idea is that rather than writing a `<meta>` tag in the `<head>` section of your markup, you could write `@viewport { width: 320px; }` in the CSS instead. This would set the browser width to 320 pixels. Some browsers already support the syntax (Opera Mobile, for example), albeit by using their own vendor prefix; for example, `@-o-viewport { width: 320px; }`.

Fixing the design for different viewport widths

With our meta viewport problem fixed, no browsers are now zooming the page, so we can set about fixing the design for different viewports. In the CSS, we'll add a media query for devices such as tablets (for example, iPad) that have a viewport width of 768 pixels in portrait view (as the landscape viewport width is 1024 pixels, it renders the page fine when loaded in Landscape view).

```
@media screen and (max-width: 768px) {
  #wrapper {
    width: 768px;
  }
  #header,#footer,#navigation {
    width: 748px;
  }
}
```

Our media query is re-sizing the width of the wrapper, header, footer, and navigation elements if the viewport size is no larger than 768 pixels. The following screenshot shows how this looks like on our iPad:

I'm actually quite encouraged by that. The content now fits on the iPad display (or any other viewport no larger than 768 pixels) with no clipping. However, we need to fix the Navigation area as the links are extending off the background image and the main content area is floating below the sidebar (as it's too wide to fit in the available space). Let's amend our media query in the CSS, as demonstrated in the following code snippet:

```
@media screen and (max-width: 768px) {
  #wrapper {
    width: 768px;
  }
  #header,#footer,#navigation {
    width: 748px;
  }
  #content,#sidebar {
    padding-right: 10px;
    padding-left: 10px;
    width: 728px;
  }
}
```

Now the sidebar and content area are filling the entire page and are nicely spaced with a little padding on either side. However, this isn't very compelling viewing. I want the content first and the sidebar second (by it's nature it's a secondary area of interest). I've made another schoolboy error here, if I'm attempting to approach this design with a truly responsive design methodology.

With responsive designs, content should always come first

We want to retain as many features of our design across multiple platforms and viewports (rather than hiding certain parts with display: none or similar) but it's also important to consider the order in which things appear. At present, due to the order of the sidebar and main content sections of our markup, the sidebar will always want to display before the main content. It's obvious that a user with a more limited viewport should get the main content before the sidebar, otherwise they'll be seeing tangentially related content before the main content itself.

We could (and perhaps should) move our content above our navigation area, too. So that those with the smallest viewports get the content before anything else. This would certainly be the logical continuation of adhering to a "content first" maxim. However, in most instances, we'd like some navigation atop each page, so I'm happier simply swapping the order of the sidebar and content area in my HTML: making the content section come before the sidebar. For example, consider the following code:

```
<div id="sidebar">
  <p>here is the sidebar</p>
</div>
<div id="content">
  <p>here is the content</p>
</div>
```

Instead of the preceding code, we have code as follows:

```
<div id="content">
  <p>here is the content</p>
</div>
<div id="sidebar">
  <p>here is the sidebar</p>
</div>
```

Although we have altered the markup, the page still looks exactly the same in larger viewports due to the float:left and float:right properties on the sidebar and content areas. However, in the iPad, our content now appears first, with our secondary content (the sidebar) afterwards.

However, with our markup structured in the correct order I've also set about adding and altering more styles, specific to the 768 pixel wide viewport. This is what the media query now looks like:

```
@media screen and (max-width: 768px) {
  #wrapper,#header,#footer,#navigation {
    width: 768px;
    margin: 0px;
  }
  #logo {
    text-align:center;
  }
  #navigation {
    text-align: center;
    background-image: none;
```

```
      border-top-color: #bfbfbf;
      border-top-style: double;
      border-top-width: 4px;
      padding-top: 20px;
    }
    #navigation ul li a {
      background-color: #dedede;
      line-height: 60px;
      font-size: 40px;
    }
    #content, #sidebar {
      margin-top: 20px;
      padding-right: 10px;
      padding-left: 10px;
      width: 728px;
    }
    .oscarMain {
      margin-right: 30px;
      margin-top: 0px;
      width: 150px;
      height: 394px;
    }
    #sidebar {
      border-right: none;
      border-top: 2px solid #e8e8e8;
      padding-top: 20px;
      margin-bottom: 20px;
    }
    .sideBlock {
      width: 46%;
      float: left;
    }
    .overHyped {
      margin-top: 0px;
      margin-left: 50px;
    }
  }
}
```

Remember, the styles added here will only affect screen devices with a viewport of 768 pixels or less. Larger viewports will ignore them. Plus, because these styles are after any existing styles, they will override them where relevant. The upshot being that larger viewports get the design they got before. Devices with a 768 pixel wide viewport, look as shown in the following screenshot:

It goes without saying, we're not going to win any design awards here but with just a few lines of CSS code within a media query, we have created an entirely different layout for a different viewport. What did we do?

First off, we reset all the content areas to the full width of the media query, as demonstrated in the following code snippet:

```
#wrapper,#header,#footer,#navigation {
    width: 768px;
    margin: 0px;
}
```

Then it was merely a matter of adding styles to alter the aesthetic layout of the elements. For example, the following code snippet changes the navigation size, layout, and background, so that it would be easier for tablet users (or any users with a viewport of 768 pixels or less) to select a navigation item:

```
#navigation {
  text-align: center;
  background-image: none;
  border-top-color: #bfbfbf;
  border-top-style: double;
  border-top-width: 4px;
  padding-top: 20px;
}
#navigation ul li a {
  background-color: #dedede;
  line-height: 60px;
  font-size: 40px;
}
```

We now have exactly the same content displayed with a different layout depending upon viewport size. Media queries are good, no? Let's have a party. While you fetch the champagne, I'll just take a look on my iPhone to see how it looks there... You can have a look at it in the following screenshot:

Media queries—only part of the solution

Oh… best put that ice back in the freezer. Clearly our work is far from over; that looks horrible on the smaller 320 pixel wide viewport of our iPhone. Our media query is doing exactly what it should, applying styles dependent upon the features of our device. The problem is however, that the media query covers a very narrow spectrum of viewports. Anything with a viewport under 768 pixels is going to experience clipping and anything between 768 and 960 pixels will experience clipping as it will get the non-media query version of the CSS styles which, as we already know, doesn't adapt once we take it below 960 pixels wide (your author rests his head in his hands and lets out a long sigh).

We need a fluid layout

Using media queries alone to change a design is fine if we have a specific known target device; we've already seen how easy it is to adapt a device to the iPad. But this strategy has severe shortcomings; namely, it isn't really future-proof. At present, when we resize our viewport, the design snaps at the points that the media queries intervene and the shape of our layout changes. However, it then remains static until the next viewport "break point" is reached. We need something better than this. Writing CSS styles specific to each and every viewport permutation doesn't make allowances for future devices and a really great design is one with some degree of future proofing built in. At this point our solution is incomplete. This is more of an adaptive design rather than the truly responsive one we want. We need our design to flex before it snaps. To make that happen we need to move from a rigid and fixed layout to a fluid layout.

Summary

In this chapter, we've learned what CSS3 media queries are, how to include them in our CSS files, and how they can help our quest to create a responsive web design. We've also learned how to make modern mobile browsers render our pages in the same manner as their desktop counterparts and touched upon the need to consider a "content first" policy when structuring our markup. We've also learned the data economies that can be made when we use images in our design in the most economical way.

However, we've also learned that media queries can only provide an adaptable web design, not a truly responsive one. Media queries are an essential component in a responsive design but a fluid layout that allows our design to flex between the break points that the media queries handle is also essential. Creating a fluid base for our layout to smooth the transition between our media query break points is what we'll be covering in the next chapter.

3
Embracing Fluid Layouts

When I first started making websites at the end of the 1990s, layout structures were table based. More often than not, all the sectioning up of screen real estate was done with percentages. For example, a left navigation column might be 20 percent whilst the main content area would be 80 percent. There weren't the vast differences in browser viewports we see today so these layouts worked and scaled well across the limited range of viewports. Nobody much cared that sentences looked a little different on one screen compared to another. However, as CSS-based designs took over, it enabled web-based designs to more closely mimic print. With that transition, for many (including myself), proportionally based layouts dwindled for many years in favor of their rigid, pixel-based counterparts.

Like all great designs and solutions, they come back around. The mini car, permed hair (I wish!), and flared jeans have all made their comebacks over the years. Now, it's time for proportional layouts to make a re-appearance.

In this chapter, we shall:

- Learn why proportional layouts are necessary for responsive design
- Convert pixel-based element widths to proportional percentages
- Convert pixel-based typography sizes to their em-based equivalent
- Understand how to find the context for any element
- Learn how to make images scale fluidly
- Learn how to serve different images to different screen sizes
- Understand how media queries can work with fluid images and layouts
- Create a responsive layout from scratch using a CSS grid system

Fixed layouts aren't future proof

As I mentioned, since the "table layout" days, I've had little call to use proportional layouts. Typically, I've been asked to code HTML and CSS that best matches a design composite that almost always measures 950-1000 pixels wide. If the layout was ever built with a proportional width (say, 90 percent), the complaints would have arrived quickly, "It looks different on my monitor". Web pages with fixed, pixel-based dimensions were the easiest way to match the fixed, pixel-based dimensions of the composite.

Even in more recent times, when using media queries to produce a tweaked version of a layout, specific to a certain popular device such as an iPad or iPhone (as we did in *Chapter 2, Media Queries: Supporting Differing Viewports*), the dimensions could still be pixel-based as the viewport was known. However, whilst many might enjoy the possibility of re-charging a client each time they need a site tweaked for today's newest gizmo, it's not exactly a future proof way of building web pages. As more and more varied viewports are being introduced, we need some way of provisioning for the unknown.

Why proportional layouts are essential for responsive designs

Whist media queries are incredibly powerful we are now aware of some limitations. Any fixed width design, using only media queries to adapt for different viewports will merely "snap" from one set of CSS media query rules to the next with no linear progression between the two. From our own experience in *Chapter 2, Media Queries: Supporting Differing Viewports*, where a viewport fell between the fixed-width ranges of our media queries (as may be the case for future unknown devices and their viewports) the design required horizontal scrolling in the browser. Instead, we want to create a design that flexes and looks good on all viewports, not just particular ones specified in a media query. I'll *cut to the chase*. (See what I did there? It's a film-based saying to match our film-based site… No? I'll get my coat…) We need to switch our fixed, pixel-based layout to a fluid proportional one. This will enable elements to scale relative to the viewport until one media query or another modifies the styling.

The symbiosis of proportional layout and media queries

I've already mentioned Ethan Marcotte's article on Responsive Web Design at A List Apart (`http://www.alistapart.com/articles/responsive-web-design/`). Whilst the tools he used (fluid layout and images, and media queries) were not new, the application and embodiment of the ideas into a single coherent methodology were. For many working in web design, his article was the genesis of new possibilities. Indeed, new ways to create web pages that offered the best of both worlds; a way to have a fluid flexible design based on a proportional layout, whilst being able to limit how far elements could flex with media queries. Putting them together forms the core of a responsive design, creating something truly greater than the sum of its parts.

Amending a design from fixed to proportional layout

Typically, for the foreseeable future, any design composite you receive or create will have fixed dimensions. Currently we measure (in pixels) the element sizes, margins, and so on within the graphics files from Photoshop, Fireworks, and so on. We then punch these dimensions directly into our CSS. The same goes for text sizes. We click on a text element in our image editor of choice, note the font size, and then enter it (again, often measured in pixels) into the relevant CSS rule. So how do we convert our fixed dimensions into proportional ones?

A formula to remember

It's possible I'm coming off too much of an Ethan Marcotte fan boy, but at this point it's essential that I provide another large tip of the hat (it should probably be a bow, maybe even a kneel) to him. In Dan Cederholm's excellent book, *Handcrafted CSS*, Mr. Marcotte contributed a chapter covering fluid grids. In it, he provided a simple and consistent formula for converting fixed width pixels into proportional percentages:

target ÷ context = result

Smells a bit like an equation to you? Fear not, when creating a responsive design, this formula soon becomes your new best friend. Rather than talk any more theory, let's put the formula to work converting the current fixed dimension for the *And the winner isn't...* site to a fluid percentage based layout.

If you remember, back in *Chapter 2, Media Queries: Supporting Differing Viewports,* we established that the basic markup structure of our site looked like this:

```
<div id="wrapper">
  <!-- the header and navigation -->
  <div id="header">
    <div id="navigation">
      <ul>
        <li><a href="#">navigation1</a></li>
        <li><a href="#">navigation2</a></li>
      </ul>
    </div>
  </div>
  <!-- the sidebar -->
  <div id="sidebar">
    <p>here is the sidebar</p>
  </div>
  <!-- the content -->
  <div id="content">
    <p>here is the content</p>
  </div>
  <!-- the footer -->
  <div id="footer">
    <p>Here is the footer</p>
  </div>
</div>
```

Content was later added but what's important to note here is the CSS we are currently using to set the widths of the main structural (header, navigation, sidebar, content, and footer) elements. Note, I've omitted many of the styling rules so we can concentrate on structure:

```
#wrapper {
  margin-right: auto;
  margin-left: auto;
  width: 960px;
}

#header {
  margin-right: 10px;
  margin-left: 10px;
  width: 940px;
}

#navigation {
```

```
    padding-bottom: 25px;
    margin-top: 26px;
    margin-left: -10px;
    padding-right: 10px;
    padding-left: 10px;
    width: 940px;
}

#navigation ul li {
    display: inline-block;
}

#content {
    margin-top: 58px;
    margin-right: 10px;
    float: right;
    width: 698px;
}

#sidebar {
    border-right-color: #e8e8e8;
    border-right-style: solid;
    border-right-width: 2px;
    margin-top: 58px;
    padding-right: 10px;
    margin-right: 10px;
    margin-left: 10px;
    float: left;
    width: 220px;
}
#footer {
    float: left;
    margin-top: 20px;
    margin-right: 10px;
    margin-left: 10px;
    clear: both;
    width: 940px;
}
```

All the values are currently set using pixels. Let's work from the outermost element and change them to proportional percentages using the *target ÷ context = result* formula.

All our content currently sits within a div with an ID of #wrapper. You can see by the CSS above that it's set with automatic margin and a width of 960 px. As the outermost div, how do we define what percentage of the viewport width it should be?

Setting a context for proportional elements

We need something to "hold" and become the context for all the proportional elements (content, sidebar, footer, and so on) we intend to contain within our design. We therefore need to set a proportional value for the width that the #wrapper should be in relation to the viewport size. For now, let's knock off a naught and roll with 96 percent and see what happens. Here's the amended rule for #wrapper:

```
#wrapper {
  margin-right: auto;
  margin-left: auto;
  width: 96%; /* Holding outermost DIV */
}
```

And here's how it looks in the browser window:

So far, so good! 96 percent actually works quite well here although we could have opted for 100 or 90 percents—whatever we felt and set the design within the viewport in the most aesthetically pleasing manner.

Now changing from fixed to proportional gets a little more complicated as we move inwards. Let's look at the header section first. Consider the formula again, *target ÷ context = result*. Our #header div (the target) sits within the #wrapper div (the context). Therefore, we take our #header (the target) width of 940 pixels, divide it by the width of the context (the #wrapper), which was 960 px and our result is .979166667. We can turn this into a percentage by moving the decimal place two digits to the right and we now have a percentage width for the header of 97.9166667. Let's add that to our CSS:

```
#header {
  margin-right: 10px;
  margin-left: 10px;
  width: 97.9166667%; /* 940 ÷ 960 */
}
```

And as both the #navigation and the #footer divs also have the same declared width, we can swap both of those pixel values to the same percentage-based rule.

Finally, before we take a peek in the browser, let's turn to the #content and #sidebar div's. As the context is still the same (960 px) we just need to divide our target size by that figure. Our #content is currently 698 px so divide that value by 960 and our answer is .727083333. Move the decimal place and we have a result of 72.7083333 percent—that's the width of the #content div in percentage terms. Our sidebar is currently 220 px but there's also a 2 px border to consider. I don't want the thickness of the right-hand border to expand or contract proportionally so that will stay at 2 px. Because of that I need to subtract some size from the width of the sidebar. So in the case of this sidebar, I have subtracted 2 px from the sidebar width and then performed the same calculation. I've divided the target (now, 218 px) by the context (960 px) and the answer is .227083333. Shift the decimal and we have a result of 22.7083333 percent for the sidebar. After amending all the pixel widths to percentages, the following is what the relevant CSS looks like:

```
#wrapper {
  margin-right: auto;
  margin-left: auto;
  width: 96%; /* Holding outermost DIV */
}

#header {
  margin-right: 10px;
  margin-left: 10px;
```

```
    width: 97.9166667%; /* 940 ÷ 960 */
  }

  #navigation {
    padding-bottom: 25px;
    margin-top: 26px;
    margin-left: -10px;
    padding-right: 10px;
    padding-left: 10px;
    width: 72.7083333%; /* 698 ÷ 960 */
  }

  #navigation ul li {
    display: inline-block;
  }

  #content {
    margin-top: 58px;
    margin-right: 10px;
    float: right;
    width: 72.7083333%; /* 698 ÷ 960 */
  }

  #sidebar {
    border-right-color: #e8e8e8;
    border-right-style: solid;
    border-right-width: 2px;
    margin-top: 58px;
    margin-right: 10px;
    margin-left: 10px;
    float: left;
    width: 22.7083333%; /* 218 ÷ 960 */
  }
  #footer {
    float: left;
    margin-top: 20px;
    margin-right: 10px;
    margin-left: 10px;
    clear: both;
    width: 97.9166667%; /* 940 ÷ 960 */
  }
```

The following screenshot shows what it looks like in Firefox with the viewport around 1000 px wide:

All good so far. Now, let's go ahead and replace all the 10 px instances used for padding and margin throughout with their proportional equivalent using the same *target ÷ context = result* formula. As all the 10 px widths have the same 960 px context, the width in percentage terms is 1.0416667 percent (10 ÷ 960).

Can't we just round the numbers?

Some critics of responsive design techniques (for example, see `http://tripleodeon.com/2010/10/not-a-mobile-web-merely-a-320px-wide-one/`) argue that entering numbers such as .550724638 em into stylesheets is daft. You may wonder yourself, why aren't these simply rounded to something more sensible? The counter argument is that it's a more accurate answer to the question being asked. Providing a browser with the most accurate answer should make it more able to display that answer in the most accurate manner. As a related aside, if you stayed awake through more than a couple math classes I'm sure you've heard of the Golden Ratio (`http://en.wikipedia.org/wiki/Golden_ratio`)? The mathematical ratio, found and used throughout almost every discipline we know, is expressed as approximately 1:1.61803398874989 (if you want it to 10,000 decimal places, knock yourself out here `http://www.maths.surrey.ac.uk/hosted-sites/R.Knott/Fibonacci/phi10000dps.txt`). Not a neat number by any means but quite an important one. If the Golden Ratio can suffer such precise measurements, I'm inclined to believe our web designs can too.

Everything still looks fine at the same viewport size. However, the navigation area isn't behaving. If I bring the viewport size in, just a little, the links start to span two lines:

Furthermore, if I expand my viewport, the margin between the links doesn't increase proportionally. Let's take a look at the CSS associated with the navigation and try and figure out why:

```
#navigation {
  padding-bottom: 25px;
  margin-top: 26px;
  margin-left: -1.0416667%; /* 10 ÷ 960 */
  padding-right: 1.0416667%; /* 10 ÷ 960 */
  padding-left: 1.0416667%; /* 10 ÷ 960 */
  width: 97.9166667%; /* 940 ÷ 960 */
  background-repeat: repeat-x;
  background-image: url(../img/atwiNavBg.png);
  border-bottom-color: #bfbfbf;
  border-bottom-style: double; border-bottom-width: 4px;
}

#navigation ul li {
    display: inline-block;
}

#navigation ul li a {
  height: 42px;
  line-height: 42px;
  margin-right: 25px;
  text-decoration: none;
  text-transform: uppercase;
  font-family: Arial, "Lucida Grande", Verdana, sans-serif;
  font-size: 27px;
   color: black;
}
```

Well, on first glance, looks like our third rule there, the #navigation ul li a, still has a pixel-based margin of 25 px. Let's go ahead and fix that with our trusty formula. As the #navigation div is based on 940 px our result should be 2.6595745 percent. So we'll change that rule to be as follows:

```
#navigation ul li a {
  height: 42px;
  line-height: 42px;
  margin-right: 2.6595745%; /* 25 ÷ 940 */
  text-decoration: none;
  text-transform: uppercase;
  font-family: Arial, "Lucida Grande", Verdana, sans-serif;
  font-size: 27px;
  color: black;
}
```

That was easy enough! Let's just check all is OK in the browser…

Oh, wait, that isn't exactly what we were gunning for. OK, the links aren't spanning two lines but we don't have the correct proportional margin value, clearly. The navigation links look like one big word, and not one I can find in my dictionary…

It's always important to remember the context

Considering our formula again (*target ÷ context = result*), it's possible to understand why this issue is occurring. Our problem here is the context. Here's the relevant markup:

```
<div id="navigation">
  <ul>
    <li><a href="#">Why?</a></li>
```

```
      <li><a href="#">Synopsis</a></li>
      <li><a href="#">Stills/Photos</a></li>
      <li><a href="#">Videos/clips</a></li>
      <li><a href="#">Quotes</a></li>
      <li><a href="#">Quiz</a></li>
   </ul>
</div>
```

As you can see our `<a href="#">` links sit within the `<li>` tags. They are the context for our proportional margin. Looking at the CSS for the `<li>` tags, we can see there are no width values set:

```
#navigation ul li { display: inline-block; }
```

As if often the case, it turns out that there are various ways of solving this problem. We could add an explicit width to the `<li>` tags but that would either have to be fixed-width pixels or a percentage of the containing element (the `navigation` div), neither of which allows any flexibility for the text that ultimately sits within them.

We could instead amend the CSS for the `<li>` tags, changing `inline-block` to be simply `inline`:

```
#navigation ul li {
   display: inline;
}
```

Opting for `display: inline;` (which stops the `<li>` elements behaving like block level elements), also makes the navigation render horizontally in earlier versions of Internet Explorer (versions 6 and 7) that have problems with `inline-block`. However, I'm a fan of `inline-block` as it gives greater control over the margins and padding for modern browsers so instead I'm going to leave the `<li>` tags as inline-blocks (and perhaps add an override style for IE 6 and IE 7, later) and instead move my percentage based margin rule from the `<a>` tag (which has no explicit context) to the containing `<li>` block instead. Here's what the amended rules now look like:

```
#navigation ul li {
  display: inline-block;
  margin-right: 2.6595745%; /* 25 ÷ 940 */
}

#navigation ul li a {
  height: 42px;
  line-height: 42px;
  text-decoration: none;
  text-transform: uppercase;
  font-family: Arial, "Lucida Grande", Verdana, sans-serif;
  font-size: 27px;
  color: black;
}
```

And the following screenshot shows how it looks in the browser with a 1200 px wide viewport:

So the navigation is getting there now, but I still have the problem of the navigation links spanning two lines as the viewport gets smaller, right until I get below 768 px wide when the media query we wrote in *Chapter 2, Media Queries: Supporting Differing Viewports*, then overrides the current navigation styles. Before we start fixing the navigation I'm going to switch all my typography sizes from fixed size pixels to the proportional unit, "ems". Once that's done we'll look at the other elephant in the room, getting our images to scale with the design.

Using ems rather than pixels for typography

In years gone by, web designers primarily used ems for sizing typography, rather than pixels, because earlier versions of Internet Explorer were unable to zoom text set in pixels. For some time, modern browsers have been able to zoom text on screen, even if the size values of the text were declared in pixels. So, why is using ems instead of pixels required or preferable? Here are two obvious reasons: firstly anyone still using Internet Explorer 6 (yes, those two) automatically gets the ability to zoom the text and secondly it makes life for you, the designer/developer, much easier. The size of an em is in relation to the size of its context. If we set a font size of 100 percent to our `<body>` tag and style all further typography using ems, they will all be affected by that initial declaration. The upshot of this being that if, having completed all the necessary typesetting, a client asks for all our fonts to be a little bigger we can merely change the body font size and all other typography changes in proportion.

Using our same *target ÷ context = result* formula, I'm going to convert every pixel based font size to ems. It's worth knowing that all modern desktop browsers use 16 px as the default font size (unless explicitly stated otherwise). Therefore, from the outset, applying any of the following rules to the body tag will provide the same result:

```
font-size: 100%;
font-size: 16px;
font-size: 1em;
```

As an example, the first pixel-based font size in our stylesheet controls the site's title, **AND THE WINNER ISN'T...** at top-left:

```
#logo {
  display: block;
  padding-top: 75px;
  color: #0d0c0c;
  text-transform: uppercase;
  font-family: Arial, "Lucida Grande", Verdana, sans-serif;
  font-size: 48px;
}

#logo span { color: #dfdada; }
```

Therefore, 48 ÷ 16 = 3. So our style changes to the following:

```
#logo {
  display: block;
  padding-top: 75px;
  color: #0d0c0c;
  text-transform: uppercase;
  font-family: Arial, "Lucida Grande", Verdana, sans-serif;
  font-size: 3em; /* 48 ÷ 16 = 3*/
}
```

You can apply this same logic throughout. If at any point things go haywire, it's probable the context for your target has changed. For example, consider the <h1> within the markup of our page:

```
<h1>Every year <span>when I watch the Oscars I'm annoyed...</span></
h1>
```

Our new em-based CSS looks like this:

```
#content h1 {
  font-family: Arial, Helvetica, Verdana, sans-serif;
  text-transform: uppercase;
  font-size: 4.3125em; } /* 69 ÷ 16 */

#content h1 span {
  display: block;
  line-height: 1.052631579em; /* 40 ÷ 38 */
  color: #757474;
  font-size: .550724638em; /* 38 ÷ 69 */
}
```

You can see here that the font size (which was 38 px) of the <span> element is in relation to the parent element (which was 69 px). Furthermore, the line-height (which was 40 px) is set in relation to the font itself (which was 38 px).

What on earth is an em?

The term **em** is simply a way of expressing the letter "M" in written form and is pronounced as such. Historically, the letter "M" was used to establish the size of a given font due to the letter "M" being the largest (widest) of the letters. Nowadays, em as a measurement defines the proportion of a given letter's width and height with respect to the point size of a given font.

So our structure is now resizing and we've switched our pixel-based type to ems. However, we still have to figure out how to scale images as the viewport resizes so let's look at that now.

Fluid images

Making images scale with a fluid layout can be achieved simply for modern browsers (including IE 7+). It's as simple as declaring the following in the CSS:

```
img {
  max-width: 100%;
}
```

This makes any images automatically scale to up to 100 percent of their containing element. Furthermore, the same attribute and property can be applied to other media. For example:

```
img,object,video,embed {
  max-width: 100%;
}
```

And they will scale too, apart from a few notable exceptions such as `<iframe>` videos from YouTube but we'll wrestle those into submission in *Chapter 4, HTML5 for Responsive Designs*. For now though, we'll concentrate on images as the principles are the same, regardless of the media.

There are some important considerations in using this approach. Firstly, it requires some forward planning—the images inserted must be large enough to scale to larger viewport sizes. This leads to a further, perhaps more important consideration. No matter the viewport size or device viewing the site, they will still have to download the large images, even though on certain devices the viewport may only need to see an image 25 percent of its actual size. This is an important bandwidth consideration in some instances so we'll revisit this second problem shortly. For now, let's just get our images scaling.

Making images scale with the viewport

Consider our sidebar with the posters of two cracking movies and two absolute stinkers (this isn't up for discussion). The markup is currently as follows:

```
<!-- the sidebar -->
  <div id="sidebar">
    <div class="sideBlock unSung">
```

```
        <h4>Unsung heroes...</h4>
        <a href="#"><img src="img/midnightRun.jpg" alt="Midnight Run"
width="99" height="135" /></a>
        <a href="#"><img src="img/wyattEarp.jpg" alt="Wyatt Earp"
width="99" height="135" /></a>
    </div>
    <div class="sideBlock overHyped">
        <h4>Overhyped nonsense...</h4>
        <a href="#"><img src="img/moulinRouge.jpg" alt="Moulin Rouge"
width="99" height="135" /></a>
        <a href="#"><img src="img/kingKong.jpg" alt="King Kong"
width="99" height="135" /></a>
    </div>
</div>
```

Although I've added the `max-width: 100%` declaration to the `img` element in my CSS, nothing has changed and the images aren't scaling as I expand the viewport:

The reason here is that I've explicitly stated both the width and height of my images in the markup:

```
<img src="img/wyattEarp.jpg" alt="Wyatt Earp" width="99" height="135" />
```

Another schoolboy error! So I'll amend the markup associated with the images, removing the height and width attributes:

```
<img src="img/wyattEarp.jpg" alt="Wyatt Earp" />
```

Let's see what that does for us by refreshing the browser window:

Well, that's certainly working! But that's introduced a further problem. Because the images are scaling to fill up to 100 percent of the width of their containing element, they're each filling the sidebar. As ever, there are various ways to fix this…

Specific rules for specific images

I could add an additional class to each image as done in the following code snippet:

```
<img class="sideImage" src="img/wyattEarp.jpg" alt="Wyatt Earp" />
```

And then set a specific rule for the width. However, instead I'm going to leave the markup as is and use CSS specificity to overrule the existing max-width rule with a further, more specific rule for my sidebar images:

```
img {
  max-width: 100%;
}

.sideBlock img {
  max-width: 45%;
}
```

The following screenshot shows how things look in the browser now:

Using CSS specificity in this way allows us to add additional control to the width of any other images or media, too. Also, in *Chapter 5, CSS3: Selectors, Typography, and Color Modes* we'll look at how CSS3's powerful new selectors let us target almost any element without the need for extra markup or introducing JavaScript frameworks such as jQuery to do our dirty work.

For the sidebar images I decided on a width of 45 percent simply because I know that I need to add a little margin between the images later, and so having two images totaling 90 percent of the width gives me a little room (10 percent) to play with.

Now that the sidebar images are working, I'll also remove the width and height attributes on the Oscar statue image in the markup. However, unless I set a proportional width value for it, it's not going to scale so I've tweaked the associated CSS to set a proportional width using good ol' trusty *target ÷ context = result*.

```
.oscarMain {
  float: left;
  margin-top: -28px;
  width: 28.9398281%; /* 698 ÷ 202 */
}
```

Putting the brakes on fluid images

So now the images are scaling nicely as the viewport expands and contracts. However, if by expanding the viewport the image scales beyond its native size, things get very ugly. Take a look at Oscar in the following screenshot, with the viewport up to 1900 px:

The `oscar.png` image is actually 202 px wide. However, with the viewport over 1900 px wide and the image scaling to fit, it's actually displaying over 300 px wide. We can easily "put the brakes on" this image by setting another more specific rule:

```
.oscarMain {
  float: left;
  margin-top: -28px;
  width: 28.9398281%; /* 698 ÷ 202 */
  max-width: 202px;
}
```

That would let the `oscar.png` image scale because of the more general image rule but never go beyond the more specific max-width property set above. Here's how the page looks with this rule set:

The incredibly versatile max-width property

Another tack to limit things expanding limitlessly would be to set a `max-width` property on our entire `#wrapper` div like this:

```
#wrapper {
  margin-right: auto;
  margin-left: auto;
  width: 96%; /* Holding outermost DIV */
  max-width: 1414px;
}
```

This means the design will scale to 96 percent of the viewport but will never expand beyond 1414 px wide (I settled on 1414 px as on most modern browsers it cuts the bunting flags off at the end of a flag rather than halfway through one). The following screenshot shows how it looks like with a viewport of around 1900 px:

Obviously these are merely options. It, however, proves the versatility of a fluid grid and how we can control the flow with just a few specific declarations.

Serving different images for different screen sizes

We have our images resizing nicely and we now understand how we can limit the display size of specific images should we choose to. However, earlier in the chapter we noted the inherent problem with scaling images. They must be physically larger than they are displayed in order to render well. If they aren't, they start to look a mess. Because of this, images, in terms of file size, are almost always bigger than they need to be given the likely display size.

Various people have tackled the problem, attempting to provide smaller images to smaller screens. The first notable example was the Filament Group's "Responsive Images" (http://filamentgroup.com/lab/responsive_images_experimenting_with_context_aware_image_sizing/). However, recently, I've switched to Matt Wilcox's "Adaptive Images" (http://adaptive-images.com). The Filament Group's solution required the image related markup to be altered. Matt's solution doesn't and automatically creates the (smaller) resized images based on the full size image already specified in the markup. This solution therefore allows images to be resized and served to the user as needed based upon a number of screen size break points. Let's jump in and get Adaptive Images up and running.

Setting up Adaptive Images

The Adaptive Images solution requires Apache 2, PHP 5.x, and GD Lib. So you'll need to be developing on an appropriate server to see the benefits. So, go ahead, download the .zip file and let's get started:

Extract the content of the ZIP file and copy the `adaptive-images.php` and `.htaccess` files into the root directory of your site. If you are already using an `.htaccess` file in your site's root directory, do not overwrite it. Instead read the additional information in the `instructions.htm` file included in the download.

Now create a folder in the root of your site called **ai-cache**.

Use your favourite FTP client to set write permissions of 777.

Now copy the following JavaScript into the `<head>` tag of each page that needs adaptive images:

```
<script>document.cookie='resolution='+Math.max(screen.width,screen.
height)+'; path=/';</script>
```

Note that if you're not using HTML5 (we'll be changing to HTML5 in the next chapter), if you want the page to validate, you'll need to add the `type` attribute. So the script should be as follows:

```
<script type="text/javascript">document.cookie='resolution='+Math.
max(screen.width,screen.height)+'; path=/';</script>
```

It's important that the JavaScript is in the head (preferably the first piece of script) because it needs to work before the page has finished loading, and before any images have been requested. Here it is added to the `<head>` section of our site in progress:

```
<!DOCTYPE html PUBLIC "-//W3C//DTD XHTML 1.0 Transitional//EN"
"http://www.w3.org/TR/xhtml1/DTD/xhtml1-transitional.dtd">
<html xmlns="http://www.w3.org/1999/xhtml">
<head>
<meta http-equiv="Content-Type" content="text/html; charset=UTF-8" />
<meta name="viewport"  content="width=device-width,initial-scale=1.0"
/>
<title>And the winner isn't…</title>
<script type="text/javascript">document.cookie='resolution='+Math.
max(screen.width,screen.height)+'; path=/';</script>
<link href="css/main.css" rel="stylesheet" type="text/css" />
</head>
```

Put background images somewhere else

In the past, I've typically placed all my images (both those used for background CSS elements and inline images inserted in the markup) in a single folder such as `images` or `img`. However, if using Adaptive Images, it's advisable that images to be used with CSS as background images (or any other images you don't want to be re-sized) be placed in a different directory. Adaptive Images by default defines a folder called `assets` to keep images you don't want resizing within. Therefore, if you want any images left alone, keep them there. If you'd like to use a different folder (or more than one) you can amend the `.htaccess` file as follows:

```
<IfModule mod_rewrite.c>
  Options +FollowSymlinks
  RewriteEngine On
```

```
# Adaptive-Images -------------------------------------------------
--------------------------------
```

```
RewriteCond %{REQUEST_URI} !assets
RewriteCond %{REQUEST_URI} !bkg
```

```
# Send any GIF, JPG, or PNG request that IS NOT stored inside one of
the above directories
# to adaptive-images.php so we can select appropriately sized
versions
RewriteRule \.(?:jpe?g|gif|png)$ adaptive-images.php
```

```
# END Adaptive-Images ----------------------------------------------
--------------------------------
</IfModule>
```

In this example, we have specified that we don't want images within assets or bkg adapting. Conversely, should you wish to explicitly state that you only want images within certain folders to be adapted, you can omit the exclamation mark from the rule. For example, if I only wanted images in a subfolder of my site, called andthewinnerisnt, I would edit the .htaccess file as follows:

```
<IfModule mod_rewrite.c>
  Options +FollowSymlinks
  RewriteEngine On
```

```
# Adaptive-Images -------------------------------------------------
--------------------------------
```

```
RewriteCond %{REQUEST_URI} andthewinnerisnt
```

```
# Send any GIF, JPG, or PNG request that IS NOT stored inside one of
the above directories
# to adaptive-images.php so we can select appropriately sized
versions
RewriteRule \.(?:jpe?g|gif|png)$ adaptive-images.php
```

```
# END Adaptive-Images ----------------------------------------------
--------------------------------
</IfModule>
```

That is all there is to it. The easiest way to check that it's up and running is to insert a large image into a page, and then visit the page with a smart phone. If you check the contents of your `ai-cache` folder with an FTP program you should see files and folders within named breakpoint folders, for example, `480` (see the following screenshot):

Adaptive Images isn't restricted to static sites. It can also be used alongside Content Management Systems and there are also workarounds for when JavaScript is unavailable. With Adaptive Images, there is a way to serve entirely different images based upon screen size, saving bandwidth overheads for devices that wouldn't see the benefit of the default full size images.

Where fluid grids and media queries come together

If you remember, earlier in the chapter, our navigation links were still spanning multiple lines at certain viewport widths. We can fix this problem with media queries. If our links fall apart at 1060 px and work again at 768 px (where our earlier media query takes over), let's set some additional font styles for the ranges in-between:

```
@media screen and (min-width: 1001px) and (max-width: 1080px) {
#navigation ul li a { font-size: 1.4em; }
}
@media screen and (min-width: 805px) and (max-width: 1000px) {
   #navigation ul li a { font-size: 1.25em; }
}
@media screen and (min-width: 769px) and (max-width: 804px) {
   #navigation ul li a { font-size: 1.1em; }
}
```

As you can see, we're changing the font size based upon the viewport width and the result is a set of navigation links that always sit on one line, throughout the range of 769 px to infinity. Evidence again of the symbiosis between media queries and fluid layouts — media queries limit the shortfalls of a fluid layout and a fluid layout eases the change from one set of defined styles within a media query to another.

CSS Grid systems

CSS Grid systems/frameworks are a potentially divisive subject. Some designers swear by them, others swear at them. In a bid to minimize hate mail, I'm going to say I sit entirely on the fence. Whilst I can understand why some developers think they are superfluous and in certain instances create extraneous code, I can also appreciate their value for rapidly prototyping layouts.

Here are a few CSS frameworks that offer varying degrees of "responsive" support:

- Semantic (http://semantic.gs)
- Skeleton (http://getskeleton.com)
- Less Framework (http://lessframework.com)
- 1140 CSS Grid (http://cssgrid.net)
- Columnal (http://www.columnal.com)

Of these, I personally favor the Columnal grid system as it has a fluid grid built-in alongside media queries and also uses similar CSS classes as 960.gs, the popular fixed-width grid system that most developers and designers are familiar with.

Alpha, Omega, and other common grid classes

Many CSS grid systems use specific CSS classes to perform everyday layout tasks. The `row` and `container` classes are self-explanatory but there are often many more. Therefore, always check any grid system's documentation for any other classes that will make life easier. For example, other typical de facto classes used in CSS Grid systems are `alpha` and `omega`—for the first and last items in a row respectively (the `alpha` and `omega` classes remove padding or margin) and `.col_x` where *x* is the number for the amount of columns the item should span (for example, `col_6` for six columns).

Rapidly building our site with a Grid system

Let's suppose we hadn't already built our fluid grid, nor had we written any media queries. We're handed the original *And the winner isn't...* homepage composite PSD and told to get the basic layout structure up and running in HTML and CSS as quickly as possible. Let's see if the Columnal grid system will help us achieve that goal.

In our original PSD, it was easy to see the layout was based on 16 columns. The Columnal grid system however only supports up to 12 columns so let's overlay 12 columns over the PSD instead of the original 16:

Having downloaded Columnal and extracted the contents of the ZIP file, we'll duplicate the existing page and then link to `columnal.css` rather than `main.css` in the `<head>`. To create visual structure using Columnal, the key is in adding the correct div classes in the markup. Here is the full markup of the page up to this point:

```
<!DOCTYPE html PUBLIC "-//W3C//DTD XHTML 1.0 Transitional//EN"
"http://www.w3.org/TR/xhtml1/DTD/xhtml1-transitional.dtd">
<html xmlns="http://www.w3.org/1999/xhtml">
<head>
<meta http-equiv="Content-Type" content="text/html; charset=UTF-8" />
<meta name="viewport"  content="width=device-width,initial-scale=1.0"
/>
<title>And the winner isn't…</title>
<script type="text/javascript">document.cookie='resolution='+Math.
max(screen.width,screen.height)+'; path=/';</script>
<link href="css/columnal.css" rel="stylesheet" type="text/css" />

</head>

<body>

<div id="wrapper">
  <!-- the header and navigation -->
  <div id="header">
    <div id="logo">And the winner is<span>n't...</span></div>
    <div id="navigation">
      <ul>
        <li><a href="#">Why?</a></li>
        <li><a href="#">Synopsis</a></li>
        <li><a href="#">Stills/Photos</a></li>
        <li><a href="#">Videos/clips</a></li>
        <li><a href="#">Quotes</a></li>
        <li><a href="#">Quiz</a></li>
      </ul>
    </div>
  </div>
  <!-- the content -->
  <div id="content">
    <img class="oscarMain" src="img/oscar.png" alt="atwi_oscar" />
    <h1>Every year <span>when I watch the Oscars I'm annoyed...</
span></h1>
    <p>that films like King Kong, Moulin Rouge and Munich get the
statue whilst the real cinematic heroes lose out. Not very Hollywood
is it?</p>
```

```
<p>We're here to put things right. </p>
  <a href="#">these should have won &raquo;</a>
  </div>
  <!-- the sidebar -->
  <div id="sidebar">
    <div class="sideBlock unSung">
      <h4>Unsung heroes...</h4>
      <a href="#"><img src="img/midnightRun.jpg" alt="Midnight Run"
/></a>
      <a href="#"><img class="sideImage" src="img/wyattEarp.jpg"
alt="Wyatt Earp" /></a>
    </div>
    <div class="sideBlock overHyped">
      <h4>Overhyped nonsense...</h4>
      <a href="#"><img src="img/moulinRouge.jpg" alt="Moulin Rouge"
/></a>
      <a href="#"><img src="img/kingKong.jpg" alt="King Kong" /></a>
    </div>
  </div>
  <!-- the footer -->
  <div id="footer">
    <p>Note: our opinion is absolutely correct. You are wrong, even if
you think you are right. That's a fact. Deal with it.</p>
  </div>

</div>
</body>
</html>
```

First of all, we need to specify that our #wrapper div is the container for all elements so we'll add the .container class to it:

```
<div id="wrapper" class="container">
```

Working down the page we can see that our **AND THE WINNER ISN'T** text is the first row. Therefore, we'll add the .row class to that element:

```
<div id="header" class="row">
```

Our logo, although just text, sits within this row and spans the entire 12 columns. Therefore we'll add .col_12 to it:

```
<div id="logo" class="col_12">And the winner is<span>n't...</span></
div>
```

Then the navigation is the next row so we'll add a .row class to that:

```
<div id="navigation" class="row">
```

And on the process goes, adding `.row` and `.col_x` classes as necessary. We'll jump ahead at this point, as I'm concerned the repetition of this process may have you nodding off. Instead, here is the entire amended markup. Note, it was also necessary to move the Oscar image and set it in its own column. Plus add a wrapping `.row` div around our `#content` and `#sidebar`.

```html
<!DOCTYPE html PUBLIC "-//W3C//DTD XHTML 1.0 Transitional//EN"
"http://www.w3.org/TR/xhtml1/DTD/xhtml1-transitional.dtd">
<html xmlns="http://www.w3.org/1999/xhtml">
<head>
<meta http-equiv="Content-Type" content="text/html; charset=UTF-8" />
<meta name="viewport"  content="width=device-width,initial-scale=1.0"
/>
<title>And the winner isn't…</title>
<script type="text/javascript">document.cookie='resolution='+Math.
max(screen.width,screen.height)+'; path=/';</script>
<link href="css/columnal.css" rel="stylesheet" type="text/css" />
<link href="css/custom.css" rel="stylesheet" type="text/css" />

</head>

<body>

<div id="wrapper" class="container">
  <!-- the header and navigation -->
  <div id="header" class="row">
    <div id="logo" class="col_12">And the winner is<span>n't...</
span></div>
    <div id="navigation" class="row">
      <ul>
        <li><a href="#">Why?</a></li>
        <li><a href="#">Synopsis</a></li>
        <li><a href="#">Stills/Photos</a></li>
        <li><a href="#">Videos/clips</a></li>
        <li><a href="#">Quotes</a></li>
        <li><a href="#">Quiz</a></li>
      </ul>
    </div>
  </div>
  <div class="row">
    <!-- the content -->
    <div id="content" class="col_9 alpha omega">
      <img class="oscarMain col_3" src="img/oscar.png" alt="atwi_
oscar" />
      <div class="col_6 omega">
      <h1>Every year <span>when I watch the Oscars I'm annoyed...</
span></h1>
```

```
        <p>that films like King Kong, Moulin Rouge and Munich get the
statue whilst the real cinematic heroes lose out. Not very Hollywood
is it?</p>
      <p>We're here to put things right. </p>
        <a href="#">these should have won &raquo;</a>
        </div>
        </div>
        <!-- the sidebar -->
        <div id="sidebar" class="col_3">
          <div class="sideBlock unSung">
            <h4>Unsung heroes...</h4>
            <a href="#"><img src="img/midnightRun.jpg" alt="Midnight Run"
/></a>
            <a href="#"><img class="sideImage" src="img/wyattEarp.jpg"
alt="Wyatt Earp" /></a>
          </div>
          <div class="sideBlock overHyped">
            <h4>Overhyped nonsense...</h4>
            <a href="#"><img src="img/moulinRouge.jpg" alt="Moulin Rouge"
/></a>
            <a href="#"><img src="img/kingKong.jpg" alt="King Kong" /></a>
          </div>
        </div>
      </div>
      <!-- the footer -->
      <div id="footer" class="row">
        <p>Note: our opinion is absolutely correct. You are wrong, even if
you think you are right. That's a fact. Deal with it.</p>
      </div>

    </div>
    </body>
    </html>
```

It was also necessary to add some extra CSS styles into a custom.css file. The content of this file is as follows:

```
#navigation ul li {
  display: inline-block;
}

#content {
  float: right;
}

#sidebar {
  float: left;
}

.sideBlock {
```

```
    width: 100%;
}

.sideBlock img {
  max-width: 45%;
  float:left;
}

.footer {
  float: left;
}
```

With these basic changes done, a quick look in the browser window shows that our basic structure is in place and scales with the browser viewport:

There's obviously a lot of detail work to still be done (I know, that's more than a slight understatement) but if you need a fast way of creating a basic responsive structure, CSS Grid systems such as Columnal are worthy of consideration.

Summary

In this chapter, we've learned how to change a rigid pixel-based structure to a flexible percentage-based one. We've also learned how to use ems, rather than pixels for more flexible typesetting. We now also understand how we can make images respond and resize fluidly as well as implementing a server-based solution for serving entirely different images based upon device screen size. Finally, we've experimented with a responsive CSS Grid system that allows us to rapidly prototype responsive structures with very minimal effort.

However, until this point we've been pursuing our responsive quest using HTML 4.01 for our markup. In *Chapter 1, Getting Started with HTML5, CSS3, and Responsive Web Design*, we touched upon some of the economies that HTML5 offers us. These economies are particularly important and relevant for responsive designs where a "mobile first" mindset lends itself to the leanest, fastest, and most semantic code possible. In the next chapter, we're going to get to grips with HTML5 and modify our markup to take advantage of the latest and greatest iteration of the HTML specification.

4
HTML5 for Responsive Designs

HTML5 evolved from the Web Applications 1.0 project, started by the **Web Hypertext Application Technology Working Group (WHATWG)** before being later embraced by the W3C. Subsequently, large parts of the specification are weighted towards dealing with web applications. If you're not building web applications, that doesn't mean there aren't plenty of things in HTML5 you could (and indeed should) embrace when embarking on a responsive design. So, whilst some features of HTML5 are directly relevant to building better responsive web pages (for example, leaner code), others are outside our responsive remit.

HTML5 also provides specific tools for handling forms and user input. This set of features takes much of the burden away from more resource heavy technologies like JavaScript for things like form validation. However, we're going to look at HTML5 forms separately in *Chapter 8, Conquer Forms with HTML5 and CSS3*.

In this chapter, we will cover the following:

- What parts of HTML5 can we use right now?
- How to write HTML5 pages
- The economies of using HTML5
- Obsolete HTML features
- New semantic HTML5 elements
- Using Web Accessibility Initiative - Accessible Rich Internet Applications (WAI-ARIA) for increased semantics and aiding assistive technologies
- Embedding media
- Responsive HTML5 and iFrame videos
- Making a website available offline

What parts of HTML5 can we use today?

Although the full specification of HTML5 is yet to be ratified, most new features of HTML5 are already supported, to varying degrees, by modern web browsers including Apple's Safari, Google Chrome, Opera, and Mozilla Firefox and even Internet Explorer 9! So, whilst it's improbable everything in the current draft of the HTML5 specification will survive until recommendation by the W3C, there are plenty of new features that can be implemented right now.

Most sites can be written in HTML5

Currently, if I'm tasked to build a website, my default markup would be HTML5 rather than HTML 4.01. Where the opposite was the case only a few years ago, at present, there has to be a compelling reason not to markup a site in HTML5. All modern browsers understand common HTML5 features with no problems (the new structural elements, video and audio tags) and older versions of IE can be served **polyfills** to address all of the shortfalls I have encountered.

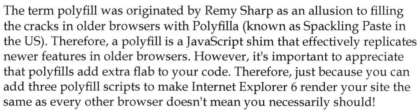

What are polyfills?

The term polyfill was originated by Remy Sharp as an allusion to filling the cracks in older browsers with Polyfilla (known as Spackling Paste in the US). Therefore, a polyfill is a JavaScript shim that effectively replicates newer features in older browsers. However, it's important to appreciate that polyfills add extra flab to your code. Therefore, just because you can add three polyfill scripts to make Internet Explorer 6 render your site the same as every other browser doesn't mean you necessarily should!

Polyfills, shims, and Modernizr

Ordinarily, older versions of Internet Explorer (pre v9) have no understanding of any of the new semantic elements of HTML5. However, some time ago, Sjoerd Visscher discovered that if elements are created with JavaScript first, Internet Explorer is able to recognize and style them accordingly. Armed with this knowledge, JavaScript whiz Remy Sharp created a lightweight enabling script (`http://remysharp.com/2009/01/07/html5-enabling-script/`) that, if included in an HTML5 page, magically switched these elements on for older versions of Internet Explorer. For a long time, pioneers of HTML5 would stick this script in their markup to enable users viewing in Internet Explorer 6, 7, and 8 to enjoy a comparable experience.

However, things have now progressed significantly. There's now a new kid on the block that does all this and a whole lot more. Its name is Modernizr (`http://www.modernizr.com`) and if you're writing pages in HTML5, it's well worth your attention. Besides enabling HTML5 structural elements for IE, it also provides the ability to conditionally load further polyfills, CSS files, and additional JavaScript files based on a number of feature tests.

So, as there are few good reasons for not using HTML5, let's get going and start writing some markup, HTML5 style.

Want a shortcut to great HTML5 code? Consider the HTML5 Boilerplate

If time is short and you need a good starting point for your project, consider using the HTML5 Boilerplate (`http://html5boilerplate.com/`). It's a pre-made "best practice" HTML5 file, including essential styles (such as the aforementioned normalize.css), polyfills, and tools such as Modernizr. It also includes a build tool that automatically concatenates CSS and JS files and strips comments to create production ready code. Highly recommended!

How to write HTML5 pages

Open an existing web page. There is a chance that the first few lines will look something like this:

```
<!DOCTYPE html PUBLIC "-//W3C//DTD XHTML 1.0 Transitional//EN"
"http://www.w3.org/TR/xhtml1/DTD/xhtml1-transitional.dtd">
<html xmlns="http://www.w3.org/1999/xhtml">
<head>
<meta http-equiv="Content-Type" content="text/html; charset=UTF-8" />
```

Delete the preceding code snippet and replace it with the following code snippet:

```
<!DOCTYPE html>
<html lang="en">
<head>
<meta charset=utf-8>
```

Save the document and you should now have your first HTML5 page as far as the W3C validator is concerned (`http://validator.w3.org/`).

Don't worry, that's not the end of the chapter! That crude exercise is merely meant to demonstrate HTML5's flexibility. It's an evolution of the markup you already write, not a revolution. We can use it to supercharge the markup that we already know how to write.

So, what did we actually do there? First of all, we stated the new HTML5 Doctype declaration:

```
<!DOCTYPE html>
```

If you're a fan of lowercase, then `<!doctype html>` is just as good. It makes no difference.

> **HTML5 Doctype—why so short?**
>
> The HTML5 `<!DOCTYPE html>` Doctype is so short that this was determined to be the shortest method of telling a browser to render the page in "standard mode". This most efficient syntax mindset is prevalent throughout much of HTML5.

After the Doctype declaration, we opened the HTML tag, specified the language, and then opened the `<head>` section:

```
<html lang="en">
<head>
```

> **Sprechen sie Deutsche?**
>
> According to the W3C specifications (http://dev.w3.org/html5/spec/Overview.html#attr-lang), the `lang` attribute specifies the primary language for the element's contents and for any of the element's attributes that contain text. If you're not writing pages in English, you'd best specify the correct language code. For example, for Japanese the HTML tag would be `<html lang="ja">`. For a full list of languages take a look at http://www.iana.org/assignments/language-subtag-registry.

Finally, we specified the character encoding. As it's a void element it doesn't require a closing tag:

```
<meta charset=utf-8>
```

Unless you have a good reason to specify otherwise, it's almost always UTF-8.

Economies of using HTML5

I remember, in school, every so often our super-mean (but actually very good) math teacher would be away. The class would breathe a collective sigh of relieve as, rather than "Mr Mean" (names have been changed to protect the innocent), the replacement was usually an easy-going and amiable man who sat quietly, leaving us to get on without shouting or constant needling. He didn't insist on silence whilst we worked, he didn't much care how elegant our workings were on the page – all that mattered was the answers. If HTML5 were a math teacher, it would be that easy-going supply teacher. I'll qualify this bizarre analogy…

If you pay attention to how you write code, you'll typically use lowercase for the most part, wrap attribute values in quotation marks, and declare a "type" for scripts and stylesheets. For example, you might link to a stylesheet like this:

```
<link href="CSS/main.css" rel="stylesheet" type="text/css" />
```

HTML5 doesn't require such detail, it's just as happy to see this:

```
<link href=CSS/main.css rel=stylesheet >
```

I know, I know. It makes me feel weird, too. There's no end tag/slash, there are no quotation marks around the attribute values, and there is no `type` declaration. However, easy going HTML5 doesn't care. The second example is just as valid as the first.

This more lax syntax applies across the whole document, not just linked CSS and JavaScript elements. For example, specify a div like this if you like:

```
<div id=wrapper>
```

That's perfectly valid HTML5. The same goes for inserting an image:

```
<img SRC=frontCarousel.png aLt=frontCarousel>
```

That's also valid HTML5. No end tag/slash, no quotes, and a mix of capitalization and lower case characters. You can even omit things such as the opening `<head>` tag and the page still validates. What would XHTML 1.0 say about this!

A sensible approach to HTML5 markup

Although we are aiming to embrace a mobile first mindset for our responsive web pages and designs, I'll admit I can't fully let go of writing what I consider the best practice markup (note, in my case that was adhering to the XHTML 1.0 markup standards which required XML syntax). It's true that we can lose some minute amounts of data from our pages by embracing these coding economies but in all honesty, if necessary, I'll make up the shortfall by leaving an image out of my design instead!

For me, the extra characters (end slashes and quotes around attribute values) are worth it for increased code legibility. When writing HTML5 documents therefore I tend to fall somewhere between the old style of writing markup (which is still valid code as far as HTML5 is concerned, although it may generate warnings in validators/conformance checkers) and the economies afforded by HTML5. To exemplify, for the CSS link above, I'd go with the following:

```
<link href="CSS/main.css" rel="stylesheet"/>
```

I've kept the closing tag and the quotation marks but omitted the `type` attribute. The point to make here is that you can find a level you're happy with yourself. HTML5 won't be shouting at you, flagging up your markup in front of the class and standing you in a corner for not validating.

All hail the mighty <a> tag

One more really handy economy in HTML5 is that we can now wrap multiple elements in an `<a>` tag. (Woohoo! About time, right?) Previously, if you wanted your markup to validate, it was necessary to wrap each element in its own `<a>` tag. For example, see the following code snippet:

```
<h2><a href="index.html">The home page</a></h2>
<p><a href="index.html">This paragraph also links to the home page</a></p>
<a href="index.html"><img src="home-image.png" alt="home-slice" /></a>
```

However, we can ditch all the individual `<a>` tags and instead wrap the group as demonstrated in the following code snippet:

```
<a href="index.html">
<h2>The home page</h2>
<p>This paragraph also links to the home page</p>
<img src="home-image.png" alt="home-slice" />
</a>
```

The only limitations to keep in mind are that, understandably, you can't wrap one `<a>` tag within another `<a>` tag and you can't wrap a form in an `<a>` tag either.

Obsolete HTML features

Besides things such as the language attributes in script links, there are some further parts of HTML you may be used to using that are now considered "obsolete" in HTML5. It's important to be aware that there are two camps of obsolete features in HTML5—conforming and non-conforming. Conforming features will still work but will generate warnings in validators. Realistically, avoid them if you can but they aren't going to make the sky fall down if you do use them. Non-conforming features may still render in certain browsers but if you use them, you are considered very, very naughty and you might not get a treat at the weekend!

An example of an obsolete but conforming feature would be using a border attribute on an image. This was historically used to stop images showing a blue border about them if they were nested inside a link. For example, see the following:

```
<img src="frontCarousel.png" alt="frontCarousel" border="0" />
```

Instead, you are advised to use CSS instead for the same effect.

In terms of obsolete and non-conforming features, there is quite a raft. I'll confess that many I have never used (some I've never even seen!). It's possible you may experience a similar reaction. However, if you're curious, you can find the full list of obsolete and non-conforming features at `http://dev.w3.org/html5/spec/Overview.html#non-conforming-features`. Notable obsolete and non-conforming features are `strike`, `center`, `font`, `acronym`, `frame`, and `frameset`.

New semantic elements in HTML5

My dictionary defines semantics as "the branch of linguistics and logic concerned with meaning". For our purposes, semantics is the process of giving our markup meaning. Why is this important? Glad you asked. Consider the structure of our current markup for the *And the winner isn't...* site:

```
<body>
<div id="wrapper">
  <div id="header">
    <div id="logo"></div>
    <div id="navigation">
      <ul>
        <li><a href="#">Why?</a></li>
      </ul>
```

```
      </div>
    </div>
    <!-- the content -->
    <div id="content">

    </div>
    <!-- the sidebar -->
    <div id="sidebar">

    </div>
    <!-- the footer -->
    <div id="footer">

    </div>
  </div>
</body>
```

Most writers of markup will see common conventions for the ID names of the div's used—header, content, sidebar, and so on. However, as far as the code itself goes, any user agent (web browser, screen reader, search engine crawler, and so on) looking at it couldn't say for sure what the purpose of each div section is. HTML5 aims to solve that problem with new semantic elements. From a structure perspective these are explained in the sections that follow.

The <section> element

The <section> element is used to define a generic section of a document or application. For example, you may choose to create sections round your content; one section for contact information, another section for news feeds, and so on. It's important to understand that it isn't intended for styling purposes. If you need to wrap an element merely to style it, you should continue to use a <div> as you would have before.

> To find out what the W3C HTML5 specification says about <section>, go to the following URL:
>
> http://dev.w3.org/html5/spec/Overview.html#the-section-element

The <nav> element

The <nav> element is used to define major navigational blocks—links to other pages or to parts within the page. As it is for use in major navigational blocks it isn't strictly intended for use in footers (although it can be) and the like, where groups of links to other pages are common.

> To find out what the W3C HTML5 specification says about <nav>, go to the following URL:
>
> http://dev.w3.org/html5/spec/Overview.html#the-nav-element

The <article> element

The <article> element, alongside <section> can easily lead to confusion. I certainly had to read and re-read the specifications of each before it sank in. The <article> element is used to wrap a self-contained piece of content. When structuring a page, ask whether the content you're intending to use within a <article> tag could be taken as a whole lump and pasted onto a different site and still make complete sense? Another way to think about it is would the content being wrapped in <article> actually constitute a separate article in a RSS feed? The obvious example of content that should be wrapped with an <article> element would be a blog post. Be aware that if nesting <article> elements, it is presumed that the nested <article> elements are principally related to the outer article.

> What the W3C HTML5 specification says about <article>:
>
> http://dev.w3.org/html5/spec/Overview.html#the-article-element

The <aside> element

The <aside> element is used for content that is tangentially related to the content around it. In practical terms, I often use it for sidebars (when it contains suitable content). It's also considered suitable for pull quotes, advertising, and groups of navigation elements (such as Blog rolls, and so on).

For more on what the W3C HTML5 specification says about `<aside>`, visit:

`http://dev.w3.org/html5/spec/Overview.html#the-aside-element`

The <hgroup> element

If you have a number of headings, taglines and subheadings in `<h1>`,`<h2>`,`<h3>`, and the subsequent tags then consider wrapping them in the `<hgroup>` tag. Doing so will hide the secondary elements from the HTML5 outline algorithm as only the first heading element within an `<hgroup>` contributes to the documents outline.

The HTML5 outline algorithm

HTML5 allows each sectioning container to have its own self-contained outline. This means it's no longer necessary to think constantly about which level of header tag you're at. For example, within a blog, I can set my post titles to use the `<h1>` tag, whilst my blog title itself also has a `<h1>` tag. For example, consider the following structure:

```
<hgroup>
  <h1>Ben's blog</h1>
  <h2>All about what I do</h2>
</hgroup>
  <article>
    <header>
      <hgroup>
        <h1>A post about something</h1>
        <h2>Trust me this is a great read</h2>
        <h3>No, not really</h3>
        <p>See. Told you.</p>
      </hgroup>
    </header>
  </article>
```

Despite having multiple `<h1>` and `<h2>` headings, the outline still appears as follows:

- Ben's blog
  - A post about something

As such, you don't need to keep track of the heading tag you need to use. You can just use whatever level of heading tag you like within each piece of sectioned content and the HTML5 outline algorithm will order it accordingly.

You can test the outline of your documents using HTML5 outliners at one the following URLs:

- `http://gsnedders.html5.org/outliner/`
- `http://hoyois.github.com/html5outliner/`

The following screenshot shows the HTML 5 Outliner page:

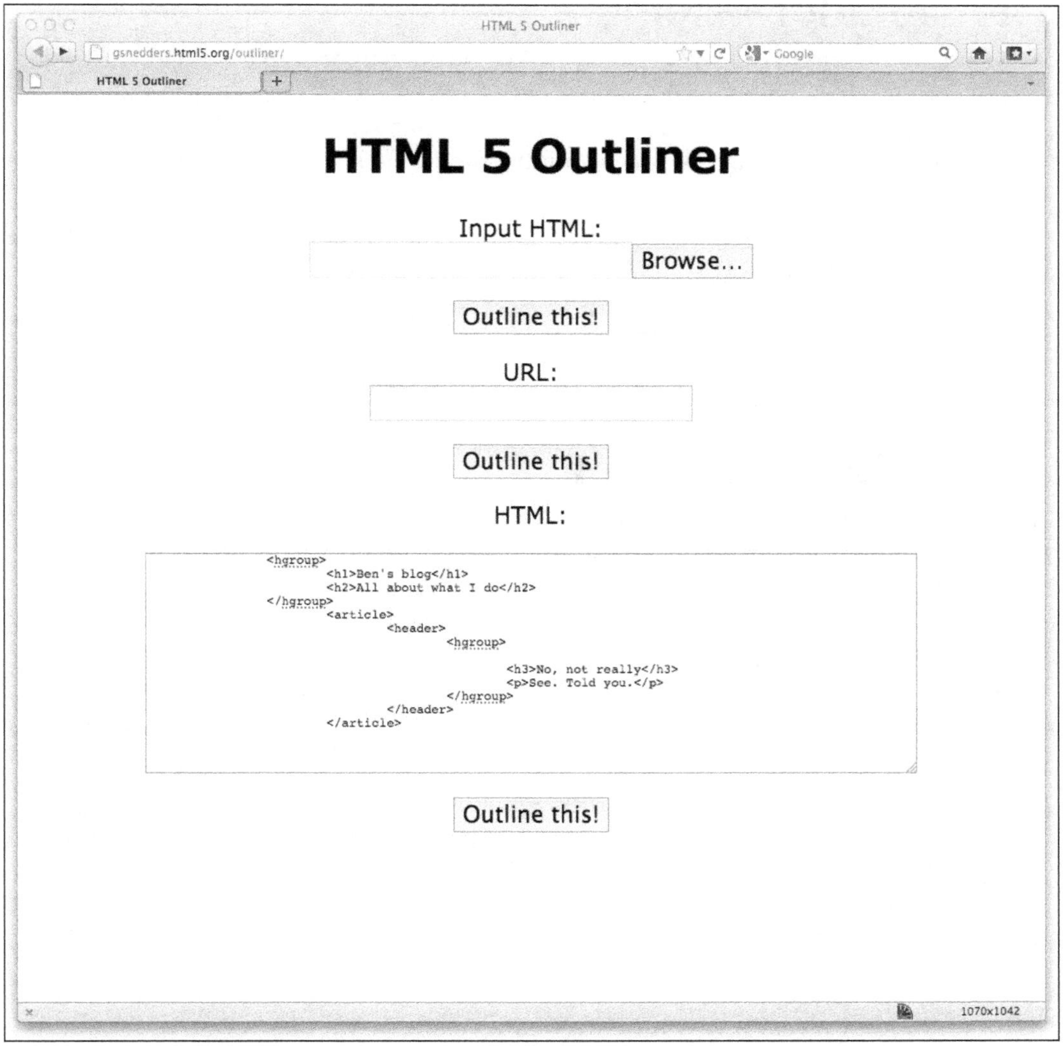

For more on what the W3C HTML5 specification says about
<hgroup>, visit:

http://dev.w3.org/html5/spec/Overview.html#the-
hgroup-element

The <header> element

The <header> element doesn't take part in the outline algorithm so can't be used to section content. Instead it should be used as an introduction to content. Practically, the <header> can be used for the "masthead" area of a site's header but also as an introduction to other content such as an introduction to a <article> element.

What the W3C HTML5 specification says about <header>:

http://dev.w3.org/html5/spec/Overview.html#the-
header-element

The <footer> element

Like the <header>, the <footer> element doesn't take part in the outline algorithm so doesn't section content. Instead it should be used to contain information about the section it sits within. It might contain links to other documents or copyright information for example. Like the <header> it can be used multiple times within a page if needed. For example, it could be used for the footer of a blog but also a footer within a blog post <article>. However, the specification notes that contact information for the author of a blog post should instead be wrapped by an<address> element.

What the W3C HTML5 specification says about <footer>:

http://dev.w3.org/html5/spec/Overview.html#the-
footer-element

The <address> element

The <address> element is to be used explicitly for marking up contact information for its nearest <article> or <body> ancestor. To confuse matters, keep in mind that it **isn't** to be used for postal addresses and the like unless they are indeed the contact addresses for the content in question. Instead postal addresses and other arbitrary contact information should be wrapped in good ol' <p> tags.

> For more on what the W3C HTML5 specification says about
> <address>:
> http://dev.w3.org/html5/spec/Overview.html#the-
> address-element

Practical usage of HTML5's structural elements

Let's look at some practical examples of these new elements. I think the <header>, <nav>, and <footer> elements are pretty self explanatory so for starters, let's take the current *And the winner isn't...* home page markup and amend the header, navigation, and footer areas (see highlighted areas in the following code snippet):

```
<!DOCTYPE html>
<html lang="en">
<head>
<meta charset=utf-8>
<meta name="viewport"  content="width=device-width,initial-scale=1.0"
/>
<title>And the winner isn't…</title>
<script>document.cookie='resolution='+Math.max(screen.width,screen.
height)+'; path=/';</script>
<link href="css/main.css" rel="stylesheet" />

</head>

<body>

<div id="wrapper">
  <!-- the header and navigation -->
  <header>
    <div id="logo">And the winner is<span>n't...</span></div>
    <nav>
      <ul>
        <li><a href="#">Why?</a></li>
        <li><a href="#">Synopsis</a></li>
```

```
            <li><a href="#">Stills/Photos</a></li>
            <li><a href="#">Videos/clips</a></li>
            <li><a href="#">Quotes</a></li>
            <li><a href="#">Quiz</a></li>
        </ul>
      </nav>
    </header>
    <!-- the content -->
    <div id="content">
        <img class="oscarMain" src="img/oscar.png" alt="atwi_oscar" />
        <h1>Every year <span>when I watch the Oscars I'm annoyed...</
span></h1>
        <p>that films like King Kong, Moulin Rouge and Munich get the
statue whilst the real cinematic heroes lose out. Not very Hollywood
is it?</p>
<p>We're here to put things right. </p>
  <a href="#">these should have won &raquo;</a>
    </div>
    <!-- the sidebar -->
    <div id="sidebar">
        <div class="sideBlock unSung">
          <h4>Unsung heroes...</h4>
          <a href="#"><img src="img/midnightRun.jpg" alt="Midnight Run"
/></a>
          <a href="#"><img class="sideImage" src="img/wyattEarp.jpg"
alt="Wyatt Earp" /></a>
        </div>
        <div class="sideBlock overHyped">
          <h4>Overhyped nonsense...</h4>
          <a href="#"><img src="img/moulinRouge.jpg" alt="Moulin Rouge"
/></a>
          <a href="#"><img src="img/kingKong.jpg" alt="King Kong" /></a>
        </div>
    </div>
    <!-- the footer -->
    <footer>
        <p>Note: our opinion is absolutely correct. You are wrong, even if
you think you are right. That's a fact. Deal with it.</p>
    </footer>

</div>
</body>
</html>
```

As we've seen however, where articles and sections exist within a page, these elements aren't restricted to one use per page. Each article or section can have its own header, footer, and navigation. For example, if we add a <article> element into our markup, it might look as follows:

```
<body>

<div id="wrapper">
  <!-- the header and navigation -->
  <header>
    <div id="logo">And the winner is<span>n't...</span></div>
    <nav>
      <ul>
        <li><a href="#">Why?</a></li>
      </ul>
    </nav>
  </header>
  <!-- the content -->
  <div id="content">
    <article>
      <header>An article about HTML5</header>
      <nav>
        <a href="1.html">related link 1</a>
        <a href="2.html">related link 2</a>
      </nav>
      <p>here is the content of the article</p>
      <footer>This was an article by Ben Frain</footer>
    </article>
```

As you can see in the preceding code, we are using a `<header>`, `<nav>`, and `<footer>` for both the page and also the article contained within it.

Let's amend our sidebar area. This is what we have at the moment in HTML 4.01 markup:

```
<!-- the sidebar -->
  <div id="sidebar">
    <div class="sideBlock unSung">
      <h4>Unsung heroes...</h4>
      <a href="#"><img src="img/midnightRun.jpg" alt="Midnight Run"
/></a>
      <a href="#"><img class="sideImage" src="img/wyattEarp.jpg"
alt="Wyatt Earp" /></a>
    </div>
    <div class="sideBlock overHyped">
      <h4>Overhyped nonsense...</h4>
      <a href="#"><img src="img/moulinRouge.jpg" alt="Moulin Rouge"
/></a>
      <a href="#"><img src="img/kingKong.jpg" alt="King Kong" /></a>
    </div>
  </div>
```

Our sidebar content is certainly "tangentially" related to the main content, so first of all, let's remove `<div id="sidebar">` and replace it with `<aside>`:

```
<!-- the sidebar -->
  <aside>
    <div class="sideBlock unSung">
      <h4>Unsung heroes...</h4>
      <a href="#"><img src="img/midnightRun.jpg" alt="Midnight Run"
/></a>
      <a href="#"><img class="sideImage" src="img/wyattEarp.jpg"
alt="Wyatt Earp" /></a>
    </div>
    <div class="sideBlock overHyped">
      <h4>Overhyped nonsense...</h4>
      <a href="#"><img src="img/moulinRouge.jpg" alt="Moulin Rouge"
/></a>
      <a href="#"><img src="img/kingKong.jpg" alt="King Kong" /></a>
    </div>
  </aside>
```

Excellent! However, if we take a look in the browser you'd be forgiven for letting a minor expletive slip out...

Talk about one step forward and two steps back! The reason is we haven't been and amended the CSS to match the new elements. Let's do that now before we proceed. We need to amend all references to #header to be simply header, all references to #navigation to be nav, and all references to #footer to be footer. For example, the first CSS rule relating to the header will change from:

```
#header {
  background-position: 0 top;
  background-repeat: repeat-x;
  background-image: url(../img/buntingSlice3Invert.png);
  margin-right: 1.0416667%; /* 10 ÷ 960 */
  margin-left: 1.0416667%; /* 10 ÷ 960 */
  width: 97.9166667%; /* 940 ÷ 960 */
}
```

To become:

```
header {
  background-position: 0 top;
  background-repeat: repeat-x;
  background-image: url(../img/buntingSlice3Invert.png);
  margin-right: 1.0416667%; /* 10 ÷ 960 */
  margin-left: 1.0416667%; /* 10 ÷ 960 */
  width: 97.9166667%; /* 940 ÷ 960 */
}
```

This was particularly easy for the header, navigation, and footer as the IDs were the same as the element we were changing them for – we merely omitted the initial '#'. The sidebar is a little different: we need to change references from #sidebar to aside instead. However, performing a "find and replace" in the code editor of your choice will help here. To clarify, rules like the following:

```
#sidebar {
}
```

Will become:

```
aside {
}
```

Even if you've written a huge CSS stylesheet, swapping the references from HTML 4.01 IDs to HTML5 elements is a fairly painless task.

> **Beware multiple elements in HTML5**
>
> Be aware that with HTML5 there may be multiple `<header>`, `<footer>`, and `<aside>` elements within a page so you may need to write more specific styles for individual instances.

Once the styles for the *And the winner isn't...* have been amended accordingly we're back in business:

Now, although we're telling user agents which section of the page is the aside, within that we have two distinct sections, **UNSUNG HEROES** and **OVERHYPED NONSENSE**. Therefore, in the interest of semantically defining those areas let's amend our code further:

```html
<!-- the sidebar -->
  <aside>
    <section>
      <div class="sideBlock unSung">
        <h4>Unsung heroes...</h4>
        <a href="#"><img src="img/midnightRun.jpg" alt="Midnight Run"
/></a>
        <a href="#"><img class="sideImage" src="img/wyattEarp.jpg"
alt="Wyatt Earp" /></a>
      </div>
    </section>
    <section>
      <div class="sideBlock overHyped">
        <h4>Overhyped nonsense...</h4>
        <a href="#"><img src="img/moulinRouge.jpg" alt="Moulin Rouge"
/></a>
        <a href="#"><img src="img/kingKong.jpg" alt="King Kong" /></a>
      </div>
    </section>
  </aside>
```

The important thing to remember is that `<section>` isn't intended for styling purposes, rather to identify a distinct, separate piece of content. Sections should normally have natural headings too, which suits our cause perfectly. Because of the HTML5 outline algorithm, we can also amend our `<h4>` tags to `<h1>` tags and it will still produce an accurate outline of our document:

What about the main content of the site?

It may surprise you that there isn't a distinct element to markup the main content of a page. However, the logic follows that as it's possible to demarcate everything else, what remains should be the main content of the page.

HTML5 text-level semantics

Besides the structural elements we've looked at, HTML5 also revises a few tags that used to be referred to as **inline** elements. The HTML5 specification now refers to these tags as text-level semantics (`http://dev.w3.org/html5/spec/Overview.html#text-level-semantics`). Let's take a look at a few common examples.

The <b> element

Although we may have often used the `<b>` element merely as a styling hook, it actually meant "make this bold". However, you can now officially use it merely as a styling hook in CSS as the HTML5 specification now declares that `<b>` is:

> *...a span of text to which attention is being drawn for utilitarian purposes without conveying any extra importance and with no implication of an alternate voice or mood, such as key words in a document abstract, product names in a review, actionable words in interactive text-driven software, or an article lede.*

The <em> element

OK, hands up, I've often used `<em>` merely as a styling hook, too. I need to mend my ways as in HTML5 it's meant to be used to:

> *...stress emphasis of its contents.*

Therefore, unless you actually want the enclosed contents to be emphasized, consider using a `<b>` tag or, where relevant, an `<i>` tag instead.

The <i> element

The HTML5 specification describes the `<i>` as:

> *...a span of text in an alternate voice or mood, or otherwise offset from the normal prose in a manner indicating a different quality of text.*

Suffice it to say, it's not to be used to merely italicize something.

Applying text-level semantics to our markup

Let's take a look at our current markup for the main content area of our home page and see if we can enhance the meaning to user agents. This is what we have currently:

```
<!-- the content -->
  <div id="content">
    <img class="oscarMain" src="img/oscar.png" alt="atwi_oscar" />
    <h1>Every year <span>when I watch the Oscars I'm annoyed...</
span></h1>
    <p>that films like King Kong, Moulin Rouge and Munich get the
statue whilst the real cinematic heroes lose out. Not very Hollywood
is it?</p>
<p>We're here to put things right. </p>
  <a href="#">these should have won &raquo;</a>
  </div>
```

We can definitely improve things here. To begin with, the `<span>` tag within our headline `<h1>` tag is semantically meaningless in that context so as we're attempting to add emphasis with our style, let's also do it with our code:

```
<h1>Every year <em>when I watch the Oscars I'm annoyed...</em></h1>
```

Let's look at our initial composite again:

We also need to style the film names differently, but they don't need to suggest a different mood or voice. Seems like the <b> tag is the perfect candidate here:

```
<p>that films like <b>King Kong</b>, <b>Moulin Rouge</b> and
<b>Munich</b> get the statue whilst the real cinematic heroes lose
out. Not very Hollywood is it?</p>
```

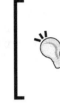

Default styling of text-level semantic elements

Because of the historical use of <b>, most browsers will still render that as bold so depending upon your situation you may need to restyle the default style in the associated CSS.

Finally, I mean it when I say 'we're here to put things right' – I'm not messing around and I want user agents to know it! So, finally, let's wrap that in a <i> tag. You could argue that I should also use the <em> tag here instead. That would also be fine in this case but I'm going with <i>. So there! This would look like the following:

```
<p><i>We're here to put things right.</i></p>
```

Like <b>, browsers will default to italicize the <i> tag so where needed, restyle as necessary.

So, we've now added some text-level semantics to our content to give greater meaning to our markup. There are plenty of other text-level semantic tags in HTML5; for the full run down, take a look at the relevant section of the specification at the following URL:

```
http://dev.w3.org/html5/spec/Overview.html#text-level-semantics
```

However, with a little extra effort we can take things one step further still by providing additional meaning for users of assistive technology.

Adding accessibility to your site with WAI-ARIA

The aim of WAI-ARIA is principally to solve the problem of making dynamic content on a page accessible. It provides a means of describing roles, states, and properties for custom widgets (dynamic sections in web applications) so that they are recognizable and usable by assistive technology users.

For example, if an onscreen widget displays a constantly updating stock price, how would a blind user accessing the page know that? WAI-ARIA attempts to solve this problem. Fully implementing ARIA is outside the scope of this book (for full information, head over to `http://www.w3.org/WAI/intro/aria`). However, there are some very easy to implement parts of ARIA that we can adopt to enhance any site written in HTML5 for users of assistive technologies.

If you're tasked with building a website for a client, there often isn't any time/money set aside for adding accessibility support beyond the basics (sadly, it's often given no thought at all). However, we can use ARIA's **landmark roles** to fix some of the glaring shortfalls in HTML's semantics and allow screen readers that support WAI-ARIA to switch between different screen regions easily.

ARIA's landmark roles

Implementing ARIA's landmark roles isn't specific to a responsive web design. However, as it's relatively simple to add partial support (that also validates as HTML5 with no further effort), there seems little point in leaving it out of any web page you write in HTML5 from this day onwards. Enough talk! Now let's see how it works.

Consider our new HTML5 navigation area:

```
<nav>
  <ul>
    <li><a href="#">Why?</a></li>
    <li><a href="#">Synopsis</a></li>
    <li><a href="#">Stills/Photos</a></li>
    <li><a href="#">Videos/clips</a></li>
    <li><a href="#">Quotes</a></li>
    <li><a href="#">Quiz</a></li>
  </ul>
</nav>
```

We can make this area easy for a WAI-ARIA capable screen reader to jump to by adding a landmark role attribute to it, as shown in the following code snippet:

```
<nav role="navigation">
  <ul>
    <li><a href="#">Why?</a></li>
    <li><a href="#">Synopsis</a></li>
    <li><a href="#">Stills/Photos</a></li>
    <li><a href="#">Videos/clips</a></li>
    <li><a href="#">Quotes</a></li>
    <li><a href="#">Quiz</a></li>
  </ul>
</nav>
```

How easy is that? There are landmark roles for the following parts of a document's structure:

- `application`: This role is used to specify a region used for a web application.
- `banner`: This role is used to specify a sitewide (rather than document specific) area. The header and logo of a site, for example.
- `complementary`: This role is used to specify an area complementary to the main section of a page. In our *And the winner isn't...* site, the **UNSUNG HEROES** and **OVERHYPED NONSENSE** areas would be considered complementary.
- `contentinfo`: This role should be used for information about the main content. For example, to display copyright information at the footer of a page.
- `form`: You guessed it, a form! However, note that if the form in question is a search form, use the `search` role, instead.
- `main`: This role is used to specify the main content of the page.
- `navigation`: This role is used to specify navigation links for the current document or related documents.
- `search`: This role is used to define an area that performs a search.

> **Taking ARIA further**
>
> ARIA isn't limited to landmark roles only. To take things further, a full list of the roles and a succinct description of their usage suitability is available at http://www.w3.org/TR/wai-aria/roles#role_definitions

Let's skip ahead and extend our current HTML5 version of the *And the winner isn't...* markup with the relevant ARIA landmark roles:

```
<body>
<div id="wrapper">
  <!-- the header and navigation -->
  <header role="banner">
    <div id="logo">And the winner is<span>n't...</span></div>
    <nav role="navigation">
      <ul>
        <li><a href="#">Why?</a></li>
        <li><a href="#">Synopsis</a></li>
        <li><a href="#">Stills/Photos</a></li>
        <li><a href="#">Videos/clips</a></li>
        <li><a href="#">Quotes</a></li>
```

```
            <li><a href="#">Quiz</a></li>
         </ul>
      </nav>
   </header>
   <!-- the content -->
   <div id="content" role="main">
      <img class="oscarMain" src="img/oscar.png" alt="atwi_oscar" />
      <h1>Every year <em>when I watch the Oscars I'm annoyed…</em></h1>
      <p>that films like <b>King Kong</b>, <b>Moulin Rouge</b> and
<b>Munich</b> get the statue whilst the real cinematic heroes lose
out. Not very Hollywood is it?</p>
<p><i>We're here to put things right.</i></p>
   <a href="#">these should have won &raquo;</a>
   </div>
   <!-- the sidebar -->
   <aside>
      <section role="complementary">
         <div class="sideBlock unSung">
            <h1>Unsung heroes...</h1>
            <a href="#"><img src="img/midnightRun.jpg" alt="Midnight Run"
/></a>
            <a href="#"><img class="sideImage" src="img/wyattEarp.jpg"
alt="Wyatt Earp" /></a>
         </div>
      </section>
      <section role="complementary">
         <div class="sideBlock overHyped">
            <h1>Overhyped nonsense...</h1>
            <a href="#"><img src="img/moulinRouge.jpg" alt="Moulin Rouge"
/></a>
            <a href="#"><img src="img/kingKong.jpg" alt="King Kong" /></a>
         </div>
      </section>
   </aside>
   <!-- the footer -->
   <footer role="contentinfo">
      <p>Note: our opinion is absolutely correct. You are wrong, even if
you think you are right. That's a fact. Deal with it.</p>
   </footer>

</div>
</body>
```

> **Test your designs for free with NonVisual Desktop Access (NVDA)**
>
> If you develop on the Windows platform and you'd like to test your ARIA enhanced designs on a screen reader, you can do so for free with NVDA. You can get it at the following URL:
>
> `http://www.nvda-project.org/`

Hopefully, this brief introduction to WAI-ARIA has demonstrated how easy it is to add partial support for those using assistive technology and you'll consider enhancing your next HTML5 project with it.

> **Styling ARIA roles**
>
> Like any attributes, it's possible to style them directly using the attribute selector. For example, you can add a CSS rule to the `navigation` role using `nav[role="navigation"] {}`.

Embedding media in HTML5

For many, HTML5 first entered their vocabulary when Apple refused to add support for Flash in their iOS devices. Flash had gained market dominance (some would argue market stranglehold) as the plugin of choice to serve up video through a web browser. However, rather than using Adobe's proprietary technology, Apple decided to rely on HTML5 instead to handle rich media rendering. Whilst HTML5 was making good headway in this area anyway, Apple's public support of HTML5 gave it a major leg up and helped its media tools gain greater traction in the wider community.

As you might imagine, Internet Explorer 8 and lower versions don't support HTML5 video and audio. However, there are easy to implement fallback workarounds for Microsoft's ailing browsers, which we'll discuss shortly. Most other modern browsers (Firefox 3.5+, Chrome 4+, Safari 4, Opera 10.5+, Internet Explorer 9+, iOS 3.2+, Opera Mobile 11+, Android 2.3+) handle it just fine.

Adding video and audio the HTML5 way

I'll be honest. I've always found adding media such as video and audio into a web page is an utter pain in HTML 4.01. It's not difficult, just messy. HTML5 makes things far easier. The syntax is much like adding an image:

```
<video src="myVideo.ogg"></video>
```

A breath of fresh air for most web designers! Rather than the abundance of code currently needed to include video in a page, HTML5 allows a single `<video></video>`tag (or `<audio></audio>` for audio) to do all the heavy lifting. It's also possible to insert text between the opening and closing tag to inform users when they aren't using an HTML5 compatible browser and there are additional attributes you'd ordinarily want to add, such as the `height` and `width`. Let's add these in:

```
<video src="video/myVideo.mp4" width="640" height="480">What, do you
mean you don't understand HTML5?</video>
```

Now, if we add the preceding code snippet into our page and look at it in Safari, it will appear but there will be no controls for playback. To get the default playback controls we need to add the `controls` attribute. We could also add the `autoplay` attribute (not recommended — it's common knowledge that everyone hates videos that auto-play). This is demonstrated in the following code snippet:

```
<video src="video/myVideo.mp4" width="640" height="480" controls
autoplay>What, do you mean you don't understand HTML5?</video>
```

The result of the preceding code snippet is shown in the following screenshot:

Further attributes include `preload` to control pre-loading of media (early HTML5 adopters should note that `preload` replaces `autobuffer`), `loop` to repeat the video, and `poster` to define a poster frame of video. This is useful if there's likely to be a delay in the video playing. To use an attribute, simply add it to the tag. Here's an example including all these attributes:

```
<video src="video/myVideo.mp4" width="640" height="480" controls
autoplay preload="auto" loop poster="myVideoPoster.jpg">What, do you
mean you don't understand HTML5?</video>
```

Providing alternate source files

The original specification for HTML5 called for all browsers to support the direct playback (without plugins) of video and audio inside Ogg containers. However, due to disputes within the HTML5 working group, the insistence on support for Ogg (including Theora video and Vorbis audio), as a baseline standard, was dropped by more recent iterations of the HTML5 specification. Therefore at present, some browsers support playback of one set of video and audio files whilst others support the other set. For example, Safari only allows MP4/H.264/AAC media to be used with the `<video>` and `<audio>` elements whilst Firefox and Opera only support Ogg and WebM.

Why can't we all just get along! (Mars Attacks)

Thankfully, there is a way to support multiple formats within one tag. It doesn't however preclude us from needing to create multiple versions of our media. Whilst we all keep our fingers crossed this situation resolves itself in due course, in the meantime, armed with multiple versions of our file, we can markup the video as follows:

```
<video width="640" height="480" controls autoplay preload="auto" loop
poster="myVideoPoster.jpg">
    <source src="video/myVideo.ogv" type="video/ogg">
    <source src="video/myVideo.mp4" type="video/mp4">
    What, do you mean you don't understand HTML5?
</video>
```

If the browser supports playback of Ogg, it will use that file; if not, it will continue down to the next `<source>` tag.

Fallback for older browsers

Using the `<source>` tag in this manner, enables us to provide a number of fallbacks, if needed. For example, alongside providing both MP4 and Ogg versions, if we wanted to ensure a suitable fallback for Internet Explorer 8 and lower versions, we could add a Flash fallback. Further still, if the user didn't have any suitable playback technology, we could provide download links to the files themselves:

```
<video width="640" height="480" controls autoplay preload="auto" loop
poster="myVideoPoster.jpg">
    <source src="video/myVideo.mp4" type="video/mp4">
    <source src="video/myVideo.ogv" type="video/ogg">
    <object width="640" height="480" type="application/x-shockwave-
flash" data="myFlashVideo.SWF">
    <param name="movie" value="myFlashVideo.swf" />
    <param name="flashvars" value="controlbar=over&amp;image=myVideoPo
ster.jpg&amp;file=video/myVideo.mp4" />
    <img src="myVideoPoster.jpg" width="640" height="480" alt="__
TITLE__"
        title="No video playback capabilities, please download the
video below" />
    </object>
    <p>  <b>Download Video:</b>
  MP4 Format:  <a href="myVideo.mp4">"MP4"</a>
  Ogg Format:  <a href="myVideo.ogv">"Ogg"</a>
    </p>
</video>
```

Audio and video tags work almost identically

The `<audio>` tag works on the same principles with the same attributes excluding width, height, and poster. Indeed, you can also use `<video>` and `<audio>` tags almost interchangeably. The main difference between the two being the fact that `<audio>` has no playback area for visible content.

Responsive video

We have seen that, as ever, supporting older browsers leads to code bloat. What began with the `<video>` tag being one or two lines ended up being 10 or more lines (and an extra Flash file) just to make older versions of Internet Explorer happy! For my own part, I'm usually happy to forego the Flash fallback in pursuit of a smaller code footprint but each usage case differs.

Now, the only problem with our lovely HTML5 video implementation is it's not responsive. That's right. All that hard work and our responsive web design doesn't err… respond. Take a look at the following screenshot and do your best to fight back the tears:

Thankfully, for HTML5 embedded video, the fix is easy. Simply remove any `height` and `width` attributes in the markup (for example, remove `width="640"` `height="480"`) and add the following in the CSS:

```
video { max-width: 100%; height: auto; }
```

However, whilst that works fine for files that we might be hosting locally, it doesn't solve the problem of videos embedded within an iFrame (take a bow YouTube, Vimeo, et al). The following code adds a film trailer for Midnight Run from YouTube:

```
<iframe width="960" height="720" src="http://www.youtube.com/embed/
B1_N28DA3gY" frameborder="0" allowfullscreen></iframe>
```

Despite my earlier CSS rule, here's what happens:

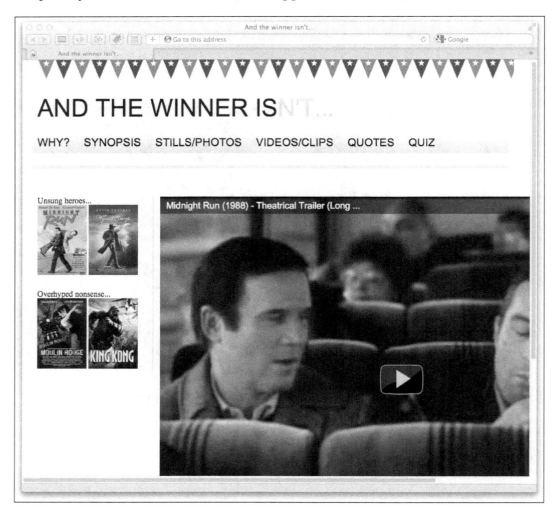

I'm sure DeNiro wouldn't be too happy about this! There are a number of ways of solving the issue, but by far the easiest I have come across is a small jQuery plugin called **FitVids**. Let's see how easy it is to use the plugin by adding it to the *And the winner isn't...* site.

First of all, we'll need the jQuery JavaScript library. Load this into your <head> element. Here, I'm using the version from Google's **Content Delivery Network (CDN)**.

```
<script src="https://ajax.googleapis.com/ajax/libs/jquery/1.6.4/
jquery.min.js"></script>
```

Download the FitVids plugin from `http://fitvidsjs.com/` (more information on the plugin is at `http://daverupert.com/2011/09/responsive-video-embeds-with-fitvids/`).

Now, save the FitVids JavaScript file into a suitable folder (I've imaginatively called mine "js") and then link to the FitVids JavaScript in the <head> element:

```
<script src="js/fitvids.js"></script>
```

Finally, we just need to use jQuery to target the particular element containing our YouTube video. Here, I've added my Midnight Run YouTube video within the #content div:

```
<script>
  $(document).ready(function(){
    // Target your .container, .wrapper, .post, etc.
    $("#content").fitVids();
  });
</script>
```

That's all there is to it. Thanks to the FitVid jQuery plugin, I now have a fully responsive YouTube video. (Note: kids, don't pay any attention to Mr. DeNiro; smoking is bad!)

Phew, all fixed. That should keep me on Bobby's Christmas card list!

Offline Web applications

Although there are plenty of exciting features within HTML5 that don't explicitly help our responsive quest (the Geolocation API, for example), Offline Web applications potentially could. As we're aware of the growing number of mobile users likely to be accessing our sites, how about we provide a means for them to view our content without even being connected to the Internet? The HTML5 Offline Web applications feature provides this possibility.

Such functionality is of most obvious use to web applications (funnily enough; wonder how they thought up the title). Imagine an online note-taking web application. A user may be halfway through completing a note when their cell phone connection drops. With HTML5 Offline Web applications, they would be able to continue writing the note whilst offline and the data could be sent once a connection is later available.

What's great about the HTML5 Offline Web applications tools is that they are too easy to set up and use. Here, we are going to use them in a basic way — to create an offline version of our site. That means that if users want to look at our site while they don't have a network connection, they can.

Offline Web applications in a nut shell

Offline Web applications work by each page that needs to be used offline, pointing to a text file known as a .manifest file. This file lists all the resources (HTML, images, JavaScript, and so on) that are needed by the page should it be offline. An Offline Web application enabled browser (Firefox 3+, Chrome 4+, Safari 4+, Opera 10.6+, iOS 3.2+, Opera Mobile 11+, Android 2.1+, Internet Explorer 10+) reads the .manifest file, downloads the resources listed, and caches them locally should the connection be dropped. Simple, eh? Let's do this...

Making web pages work offline

In the opening HTML tag, we point to a .manifest file:

```
<html lang="en" manifest="/offline.manifest">
```

You can call this file anything you want but it is recommended that the file extension used is .manifest.

You must add the `manifest="/offline.manifest"` attribute to the HTML tag of every page you want to be available offline.

If your web server runs on Apache, you'll probably need to amend the `.htaccess` file with the following line:

```
AddType text/cache-manifest .manifest
```

This will allow the file to have the correct MIME type, which is `text/cache-manifest`.

While we're in the `.htaccess` file, also add the following:

```
<Files offline.manifest>
  ExpiresActive On
  ExpiresDefault "access"
</Files>
```

Adding the preceding lines of code, stops the browser from caching the cache. Yes, you read that right. As the `offline.manifest` file is a static file, by default the browser will cache the `offline.manifest` file. So, this tells the server to tell the browser not to!

Now we need to write the `offline.manifest` file. This will instruct the browser about which files to make available offline. Here's the content of the `offline.manifest` file for the *And the winner isn't...* site:

```
CACHE MANIFEST
#v1

CACHE:
basic_page_layout_ch4.html
css/main.css
img/atwiNavBg.png
img/kingHong.jpg
img/midnightRun.jpg
img/moulinRouge.jpg
img/oscar.png
img/wyattEarp.jpg
img/buntingSlice3Invert.png
img/buntingSlice3.png

NETWORK:
*

FALLBACK:
/ /offline.html
```

Understanding the manifest file

The manifest file must begin with CACHE MANIFEST. The next line is merely a comment, stating the version number of the manifest file. More on that shortly.

The CACHE: section lists the files that we need for offline use. These should be relative to the offline.manifest file, so paths may need to be changed depending upon the resources that need caching. It's also possible to use absolute URLs if needed.

The NETWORK: section lists any resources that should not be cached. Think of it as an "online whitelist". Whatever is listed here will always by-pass the cache if a network connection is available. If you want to make your site content available where a network is available (rather than only looking in the offline cache), the * character allows it. It's known as the **online whitelist wildcard flag**.

The FALLBACK: section uses the / character to define a URL pattern. It basically asks "is this page in the cache?" If it finds the page there, great, it displays it. If not, it shows the user the file specified—offline.html.

Automatic loading of pages to the offline manifest

Depending on the circumstances, there's an even easier way of setting an offline.manifest file up. Any page that points to an offline manifest file (remember that we do this by adding manifest="/offline.manifest" in our opening <html> tag) gets automatically added to the cache when a user visits it. This technique will add every page on your site that a user visits to their cache so they can view it again offline. Here's what the manifest should look like:

```
CACHE MANIFEST
# Cache Manifest v1
FALLBACK:
/ /offline.html
NETWORK:
*
```

One point of note when opting for this technique is that just the HTML of the page that is visited will be downloaded and cached. Not the images/JavaScript and other resources it may contain and link to. If these are essential, specify them in a CACHE: section as already described earlier in the *Understanding the manifest file* section.

About that version comment

When you make changes to your site or any of its resources, you must change the `offline.manifest` file somehow and re-upload it. This will enable the server to provide the new file to the browser, which will then get the new versions of the files and kick off the offline process again. I follow Nick Pilgrim's example (from the excellent *Dive into HTML5*) and add a comment to the top of the `offline.manifest` file that I increment with each change:

```
# Cache Manifest v1
```

Viewing the site offline

Now, it's time to test our handiwork. Visit the page in an Offline Web application capable browser. Some browsers will warn about offline mode (Firefox for example—note the top bar) whilst Chrome makes no mention of it:

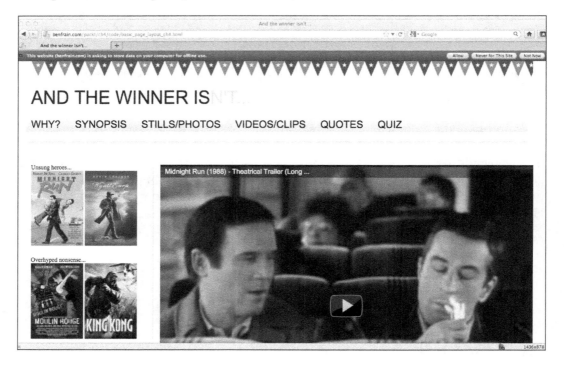

Now, pull the plug (or you know, switch off WiFi—that just didn't sound as dramatic as "pull the plug") and refresh the browser. Hopefully, the page will refresh as if connected – only it isn't.

Troubleshooting Offline Web applications

When I have problems getting sites to work correctly in Offline mode I tend to use Chrome to troubleshoot. The built-in Developer tools have a handy Console section (access it by clicking the spanner logo to the right of the address bar and then go to **Tools | Developer tools** and click the **Console** tab) that flags up success or failure of the offline cache and often points out what you're doing wrong. In my experience, it's usually path issues; for example, not pointing my pages to the correct location of the manifest file.

For the full specification of the Offline Web applications, head over to the following URL:

```
http://dev.w3.org/html5/spec/Overview.html#offline
```

Summary

We've covered a lot in this chapter. Everything from the basics of creating a page that validates as HTML5, to enabling our pages to work offline when users are lacking an Internet connection. We've also tackled embedding rich media (video) into our markup, and ensured it behaves responsively for differing viewports. Although not specific to responsive designs, we've also covered how we can write semantically rich and meaningful code and also provide help to users that rely on assistive technologies. However, our site is still facing some major shortfalls. Without putting too fine a point on it—it looks pretty shabby. Our text is un-styled and we're completely lacking details such as the buttons visible in the original composite. We've avoided loading the markup with images to solve these issues thus far with good reason. We don't need them! Instead, in the next few chapters we're going to embrace the power and flexibility of CSS3 to create a faster and more maintainable responsive design.

5
CSS3: Selectors, Typography, and Color Modes

In *Chapter 1, Getting Started with HTML5, CSS3, and Responsive Web Design*, we noted that the number of people viewing websites over mobile telecom networks is ever increasing. As current telecom network speeds vary enormously, we need to consider the bandwidth and therefore load time of the websites we build. Back in the day we had to consider how long our pages and the images and media they contained would take to load over a 56K modem. Now, we face similar loading time challenges. Just as the percentage rules of table-based layouts are re-emerging, so is the need to re-examine every piece of media and bandwidth sapping content we add to our pages. Although our devices are now mobile, the speeds they download content and the premium they face for doing so (speed and cost) is comparable to years gone by. Everything old is new again! Thankfully, CSS3 can heavily reduce our reliance on images for visual flair giving us the tools to create beautiful sites that also download in record time. There's lots of CSS3 for us to cover. *Chapter 6, Stunning Aesthetics with CSS3*, will deal with more specific CSS3 techniques including text shadows, box shadows, gradients, and backgrounds whilst *Chapter 7, CSS3 Transitions, Transformations, and Animations*, will look at CSS3 animations, transforms, and transitions.

In this chapter, we will learn the following CSS3 fundamental:

- What CSS3 offers the frontend developer
- Quick and handy CSS3 tricks (multiple columns and word wraps)
- The anatomy of a CSS rule
- What vendor-specific prefixes are and how to use them
- New CSS3 selectors and how they work
- Custom typography with `@font-face`
- How to use RGB and HSL color modes with Alpha tranparency

What CSS3 offers the frontend developer

In the past, we either gambled that users would put up with long load times for the sake of a great design (they wouldn't, by the way!) or we ditched images, often compromising our design ideals, for the sake of usability. CSS3, in many ways negates the need for compromise. With just a few lines of code (and no images!) CSS3 can produce onscreen elements such as rounded corners, background gradients, text shadows, box shadows, custom typography, and multiple background images (alright, granted, that one does require images). If that wasn't enough, much of the basic interaction for which we have previously relied on JavaScript, such as hover state animations, can also be handled with pure CSS3. There are heaps of CSS3 goodies and economies that will elevate our responsive design from merely "a normal website made responsive" to a responsive website built for the future. By utilizing CSS3, we will enable our responsive design to load faster, require less resource and be far easier to maintain and amend in the future. Before we get into that, let's deal with the "Elephant in the room".

CSS3 support in Internet Explorer versions 6 to 8

With a few exceptions (such as @font-face), few features of the new CSS3 modules are supported by Old IE (Internet Explorer versions 6, 7, and 8). Should you use CSS3 in your design? As ever in web development, the answer is "it depends".

Personally, at present, I principally use CSS3 to enhance a site, rather than provide essential functionality. I'm entirely comfortable with elements looking a little different in different browsers. I believe you and your clients should be too. You might find it helpful to refer back to the *Educating our clients that websites shouldn't look the same in all browsers* section in *Chapter 1, Getting Started with HTML5, CSS3, and Responsive Web Design*. Which parts of a design are critical to it "working" or "looking right" is subjective. But it's worth knowing that there are many polyfills available for adding CSS3 functionality to Old IE. Applying such polyfills, should you choose to follow that path, is discussed more in *Chapter 9, Solving Cross-browser Responsive Challenges*.

 For a full list of what CSS 2.1 and CSS3 features are supported in the differing versions of Internet Explorer, head over to the following URL:
`http://msdn.microsoft.com/en-us/library/`
`cc351024%28v=vs.85%29.aspx`

Using CSS3 to design and develop pages in the browser

I can't speak for you but I find re-making images tiresome. You know the kind of comment I'm talking about, "Could we make those corners a little rounder?" or "Can the gradient be a little darker at the top?" Once we've dutifully made the amends, we often hear the inevitable, "Oh, no, it was better the way it was. Can you swap it back?" Now, of course, this to-and-fro process is necessary; after all, we often want to tweak a design just to see how it looks. However, CSS3 lets you do much of this in mere seconds, within the code, rather than minutes within the graphics editor.

Anatomy of a CSS rule

Before exploring some of what CSS3 has to offer, to prevent confusion, let's establish the terminology we use to describe a CSS rule. Consider the following example:

```
.round {
  border-radius: 10px;
}
```

This rule is made up of the **selector** (.round) and then the **declaration** (border-radius: 10px;). However, the declaration is further defined by the **property** (border-radius:) and the **value** (10px;). Happy, we're on the same page? Great, let's press on.

Vendor prefixes and how to use them

As the CSS3 Modules specifications have yet to be either ratified by the W3C or have all their proposed features fully implemented into browsers, browser vendors use what's known as **vendor prefixes** to test new "experimental" CSS features. Whilst this helps browser makers implement the new CSS3 modules, it makes our lives, as writers of CSS3, just a little more tedious. Consider the following code for a rounded corner in CSS3:

```
.round{
  -khtml-border-radius: 10px; /* Konqueror */
  -rim-border-radius: 10px; /* RIM */
  -ms-border-radius: 10px; /* Microsoft */
  -o-border-radius: 10px; /* Opera */
  -moz-border-radius: 10px; /* Mozilla (e.g Firefox) */
  -webkit-border-radius: 10px; /* Webkit (e.g. Safari and Chrome) */
  border-radius: 10px; /* W3C */
}
```

You can see a number of vendor prefixed properties (and that is by no means an exhaustive list), each with their own unique prefix, for example, `-webkit-` for Webkit based browsers, `-ms-` is the Microsoft prefix, so covers the Internet Explorer, and so on. Due to the way CSS works, a browser will go line by line down the stylesheet, applying properties that apply to it and ignoring ones that don't.

Furthermore, applicable properties later in the stylesheet take precedence over earlier ones. Thanks to this cascade, we can list our vendor-prefixed properties first and then the correct (but perhaps yet to be implemented) non-prefix version last, safe in the knowledge that when the feature is fully implemented, the correct version will be implemented by the browser, rather than the experimental, browser-specific one listed before it.

Clippings and JavaScript for quick CSS3 prefixes

You may find it handy to keep clippings of common CSS3 rules containing all the necessary vendor prefixed properties. That way you can just paste them in without needing rewrite them all each time. Many code-editing programs (or **Integrated Development Environments (IDEs)** as they are often labeled) have code clip features and when using CSS3 they can save a lot of time. There's also JavaScript solutions that automatically add prefixes to CSS files, check out "-prefix-free", a great solution, at `http://leaverou.github.com/prefixfree/`.

It's acceptable to list every vendor prefix version of a property. However, in reality, few people do. Instead they either target the browsers they expect to see most often or check what browsers support the feature before writing the rule. For example, you might just opt to go with:

```
.round{
  -moz-border-radius: 10px; /* Mozilla (e.g Firefox) */
  -webkit-border-radius: 10px; /* Webkit (e.g. Safari and Chrome) */
  border-radius: 10px; /* W3C */
}
```

That would cover Firefox, Chrome, and Safari, along with any browser that has fully implemented the rule.

I know what you're thinking, isn't listing multiple vendor prefixed versions of the same property going to lead to code bloat? Well, a little yes. But no matter how many prefixed properties we add, it's still a faster, more elegant and robust solution than using images.

Before working on a site, it's wise to look at the current browser usage statistics. In doing so, you'll have a better idea of what browsers you need to build specific support for. For example, if time and budget are tight, you might decide to omit vendor specific prefixes for any browser with less than 3 percent usage rate for your site. As ever, you need to make a judgment based on a number of variables.

Now, we understand what the prefixes are and how to apply them in our rules. Let's look at some quick and useful little CSS3 tricks.

When can I use specific CSS3 and HTML5 features?

As we delve into CSS3 more and more, I can heartily recommend visiting http://caniuse.com, if you ever want to know what the current level of browser support is available for a particular CSS3 or HTML5 feature. Alongside showing browser version support (searchable by feature) it also provides the most recent set of global usage statistics from http://gs.statcounter.com.

Quick and useful CSS3 tricks

In my day-to-day work, some of the new CSS3 features I use constantly and others I've never needed. Before getting into the heavier stuff, I thought it might be useful to share a couple of CSS3 goodies that make life easier, especially in responsive designs, by accomplishing simple tasks that used to be minor headaches.

CSS3 multiple columns for responsive designs

Ever needed to make a single piece of text appear in multiple columns? Until CSS3, you'd need to separate the content into different markup elements and then style accordingly. Altering markup for stylistic purposes is never a good practice. CSS3 allows us to span one or more pieces of content across multiple columns. Consider the following markup:

```
<div id="main" role="main">
    <p>lloremipsimLoremipsum dolor sit amet, consectetur
// LOTS MORE TEXT //
</p>
    <p>lloremipsimLoremipsum dolor sit amet, consectetur
// LOTS MORE TEXT //
</p>
</div>
```

You can make all that content flow across multiple columns that are either: a certain column width (for example, 12em) or certain number of columns (for example, 3). Here's how:

For a certain width of column, use the following syntax (note that vendor prefixes have been omitted for brevity):

```
#main {
  column-width: 12em;
}
```

This will mean, no matter the viewport size, the content will span across columns that are 12 em in width. Altering the viewport will adjust the number of columns displayed dynamically.

For example, here it is in Safari with a 1024 px wide viewport:

And the following screenshot shows how the same page renders on an iPad with a 768 px wide viewport:

A beautifully responsive layout requiring the minimum of work—I like it!

If you'd rather keep a fixed number of columns and vary the width, you can write a rule like the following:

```
#main {
  column-count: 4;
}
```

Adding a gap and column divider

We can take things even further by adding a specified gap for the columns and a divider:

```
#main {
  column-gap: 2em;
  column-rule: thin dotted #999;
  column-width: 12em;
}
```

This gives us a result like the following:

To read the specification on the CSS3 Multi-column Layout Module, visit
`http://www.w3.org/TR/css3-multicol/`.

For the time being, remember you'll need to use vendor prefixes on the column
declarations for maximum compatibility.

Word wrapping

How many times have you had to add a big URL into a tiny space and, well,
despaired? Take a look at the problem in the following screenshot; notice the URL at
the bottom right breaking out of its allocated space:

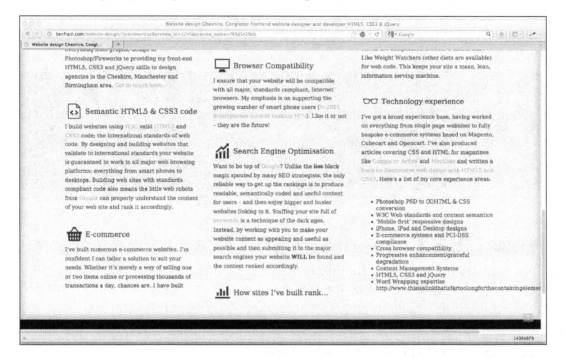

CSS3 fixes this problem with a simple declaration, which as chance would have it,
also works in older versions of Internet Explorer as far back as 5.5!

```
word-wrap: break-word;
```

Adding this to the containing element gives an effect as shown in the following screenshot. Hey presto, the long URL now wraps perfectly!

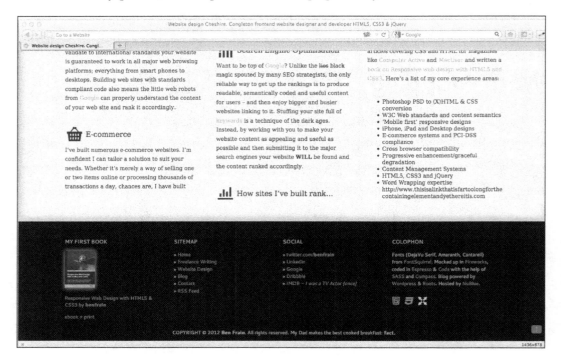

New CSS3 selectors and how to use them

CSS3 gives incredible power for selecting elements within a page. You may not think this sounds very glitzy but trust me, it will make your life easier and you'll love CSS3 for it! I'd better qualify that bold claim…

CSS3 attribute selectors

You've perhaps used existing CSS attribute selectors to target rules. For example, consider the following rule:

```
img[alt] {
  border: 3px dashed #e15f5f;
}
```

This would target any image tags in the markup which have an `alt` attribute:

```
<img class="oscarMain" src="img/oscar.png" alt="atwi_oscar" />
```

You can also narrow things down by specifying what the attribute value is. For example, consider the following rule:

```
img[alt="atwi_oscar"] {
  border: 3px dashed #e15f5f;
}
```

This would only target images which have an `alt` attribute of `atwi_oscar`. So far, so big deal we could do that in CSS2. What is CSS3 bringing to the party? Principally, three new "substring matching" attribute selectors…

CSS3 substring matching attribute selectors

CSS3 lets us select elements based upon the substring of their attribute selector. That sounds complicated. It isn't! We can now select an element, based on the contents of the attribute. The three options are whether the attribute is:

- Beginning with the prefix
- Contains an instance of
- Ends with the suffix

Let's see what they look like.

The "beginning with" substring matching attribute selector

The "beginning with" substring matching attribute selector has the following syntax:

```
Element[attribute^="value"]
```

In practical use, if I want to select all images on the site that had an `alt` attribute that *began with* `film`, I would write the following rule:

```
img[alt^="film"] {
    border: 3px dashed #e15f5f;
}
```

The key character in all this is the ^ symbol which means "begins with".

The "contains an instance of" substring matching attribute selector

The "contains an instance of" substring matching attribute selector has the following syntax:

```
Element[attribute*="value"]
```

In practical use, if I want to select all images on the site that had an alt attribute that *contained* `film` I would write the following rule:

```
img[alt*="film"] {
  border: 3px dashed #e15f5f;
}
```

The key character in all this is the * symbol which means "contains".

The "ends with" substring matching attribute selector

The " ends with " substring matching attribute selector has the following syntax:

```
Element[attribute$="value"]
```

In practical use, if I want to select all images on the site that had an alt attribute that *ended with* `film` I would write the following rule:

```
img[alt$="film"] {
  border: 3px dashed #e15f5f;
}
```

The key character in all this is the $ symbol which means "ends with".

A practical, real world example

How can these substring attribute selectors actually help? Let me give you an example where I often use CSS3 attribute selectors. If I build a website with a Content Management System (for example, Wordpress, Concrete, or Magento), it often gives the client the ability to add new pages. For example, perhaps they are adding a piece of news about their company or a product update. Each time they add a page in the CMS, the generated HTML will include an ID value for the <body> or other relevant tag, which helps distinguish the page, markup wise, from others. For example, one client was involved in Motorsport and had a "Racing History" section with yearly reports. Each <body> tag would have an ID for the year:

```
<body id="2003">
```

> **IDs can start with numbers in HTML5**
>
> If you're not used to coding in HTML5, you might assume that an ID beginning with a number is invalid, as it was in HTML 4.01. However, HTML5 removes that restriction, the only things to remember with ID names in HTML5 is that there should be no spaces in the ID name and it must be unique on the page. For more information visit http://dev.w3.org/html5/spec/Overview.html#the-id-attribute.

I needed the navigation bar link for "Racing History" to be highlighted when any of these yearly pages were viewed, as they related to the "Racing History" section. However, rather than write a style rule covering every future year, I was able to write a defensive (they are sometimes referred to as "defensive" rules as they try and safeguard against future events) CSS3 rule:

```
body[id^="2"] .navHistory { color: #00b4ff; }
```

This means that any element with a class of `.navHistory`, that is a descendant of a body with an ID beginning with 2 (for example, 2002, 2003, 2004, and on) will be colored with the hex value of `#00b4ff`. One simple rule covers all eventualities. Unless of course the website is still in its current form by the year 3000—in which case, chances are, even if I eat and exercise well, I won't be able to continue its upkeep...

CSS3 structural pseudo-classes

The more often you code websites, the more often it's likely you'll need to solve the same problem again and again. Let's consider a typical example. Horizontal navigation bars are often made up of a number of equally spaced `<li>` links. Suppose we need margin to the left and right side of each list item, except for the first and last list item. Historically, we have been able to solve this problem by adding a semantically superfluous classname to the first and last `<li>` elements in the list, as shown in the highlighted lines in the following code snippet:

```
<ul>
  <li class="first"><a href="#">Why?</a></li>
  <li><a href="#">Synopsis</a></li>
  <li><a href="#">Stills/Photos</a></li>
  <li><a href="#">Videos/clips</a></li>
  <li><a href="#">Quotes</a></li>
  <li class="last"><a href="#">Quiz</a></li>
</ul>
```

And then by adding a couple of rules in the CSS, we can amend the margin for those two list items:

```
li {
  margin-left: 5%;
  margin-right: 5%;
}
.first {
  margin-left: 0px;
}
.last {
  margin-right: 0px;
}
```

This works but isn't flexible. For example, when building a website built on a CMS system, list items for linking new content might be added automatically, so it might not be a simple task to add or remove the `last` or `first` class to the correct list item in the markup.

The :last-child selector

CSS2.1 already had a selector applicable for the first item in a list:

```
li:first-child
```

However, CSS3 adds a selector that can also match the last:

```
li:last-child
```

Using these selectors together, we don't need any additional classes in our markup.

We'll fix up our *And the winner isn't...* site navigation using this and a combination of the `display: table` property. The following screenshot shows how things look currently:

Now, let's take a look at the graphic mockup:

The navigation bar links span the full width of the design, which we need to replicate. Our markup for the navigation looks like this:

```
<nav role="navigation">
  <ul>
    <li><a href="#">Why?</a></li>
    <li><a href="#">Synopsis</a></li>
    <li><a href="#">Stills/Photos</a></li>
    <li><a href="#">Videos/clips</a></li>
    <li><a href="#">Quotes</a></li>
    <li><a href="#">Quiz</a></li>
  </ul>
</nav>
```

First, we'll set the nav element to be a `table`:

```
nav {
  display: table;
  /* more code... */
}
```

Then the `<ul>` to be displayed as a `table-row`:

```
nav ul {
  display: table-row;
  /* more code... */
}
```

And finally the list-items to display as `table-cells`:

```
nav ul li {
  display: table-cell;
  /* more code... */
}
```

This means that if extra list items are added, they will automatically space themselves accordingly. Finally, we'll use our CSS selectors to align the text to the right and left of the first and last list items:

```
nav ul li:last-child {
  text-align: right;
}

nav ul li:first-child {
  text-align: left;
}
```

Then in the browser, our navigation is approaching our original composite:

Don't worry; these tables are only for display!

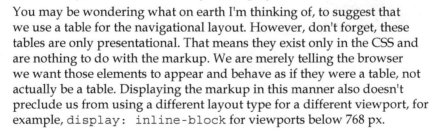

You may be wondering what on earth I'm thinking of, to suggest that we use a table for the navigational layout. However, don't forget, these tables are only presentational. That means they exist only in the CSS and are nothing to do with the markup. We are merely telling the browser we want those elements to appear and behave as if they were a table, not actually be a table. Displaying the markup in this manner also doesn't preclude us from using a different layout type for a different viewport, for example, `display: inline-block` for viewports below 768 px.

The nth-child selectors

But what about those alternate colors shown in the navigation bar links of the original composite? Again, CSS3 has a selector that can solve this problem for us without the need for additional markup:

```
:nth-child(even)
```

Let's use this selector to fix the problem and then we can look at some of the many ways that nth-child can solve problems that previously required extra markup. I'll add alternate red links in the navigation bar by adding the following style rule:

```
nav ul li:nth-child(even) a {
  color: #fe0208;
}
```

And now we have alternate colors in the navigation links:

How about that? Not a line of jQuery in site and no extra markup! What did I tell you? CSS3 selectors are great!

Understanding what nth rules do

Amongst frontend web developers and designers, nothing makes mathematics weaklings tremble quite like the **nth-based rules** (well, you know, except maybe someone asking you to code a little PHP or give them a hand with some REGEX expressions). Let's see if we can make sense of the beast and gain a little respect from those backend wizards.

When it comes to selecting elements in the tree structure of the DOM (Document Object Model or more simplistically, the elements in a page's markup) CSS3 gives us incredible flexibility with a few nth-based rules— `:nth-child(n)`, `:nth-last-child(n)`, `:nth-of-type(n)`, and `:nth-last-of-type(n)`. We've seen that we can use `(odd)` or `(even)` values (as we have to fix our navigation above) but the `(n)` parameter can be used in another couple of ways:

- Used as an integer; for example, `:nth-child(2)` — would select the second item
- Used as a numeric expression; for example, `:nth-child(3n+1)` — would start at `1` and then select every third element

The integer based property is easy enough to understand, just enter the element number you want to select. The numeric expression version of the selector is the part that can be a little baffling for mere mortals. Let's break it down. For practicality, within the brackets, I start from the right. So, for example, if I want to figure out what `(2n+3)` will select, I start at the right (from the third item) and know it will select every second element from that point on. I've amended our navigation rule to illustrate this:

```
nav ul li:nth-child(2n+3) a {
  color: #fe0208;
}
```

As you can see, the third list item is colored and then every subsequent second one after that (if there were 100 list items, it would continue selecting every second list item):

How about selecting everything from the second item onwards? Well, although you could write `:nth-child(1n+2)`, you don't actually need the first number 1 as unless otherwise stated, n is equal to 1. We can therefore just write `:nth-child(n+2)`. Likewise, if we wanted to select every third element, rather than write `:nth-child(3n+3)`, we can just write `:nth-child(3n)` as every third item would begin at the third item anyway, without needing to explicitly state it.

The expression can also use negative numbers for example, `:nth-child(3n-2)` starts at minus 2 and then selects every third item. Here's our navigation amended with the following rule:

```
nav ul li:nth-child(3n-2) a {
  color: #fe0208;
}
```

And here's what it gives us in the browser:

Hopefully, that's making perfect sense now?

The `child` and `last-child` differ in that the `last-child` variant works from the opposite end of the document tree. For example, `:nth-last-child(-n+3)` starts at 3 from the end and then selects all the items after it. Here's what that rule gives us in the browser:

Finally, let's consider :nth-last-of-type. Whilst the previous examples count any children regardless of type, :nth-last-of-type let's you be specific about the type of item you want to select. Consider the following markup:

```
<ul>
  <li class="internal"><a href="#">Why?</a></li>
  <li><a href="#">Synopsis</a></li>
  <li class="internal"><a href="#">Stills/Photos</a></li>
  <li class="internal"><a href="#">Videos/clips</a></li>
  <li class="internal"><a href="#">Quotes</a></li>
  <li class="internal"><a href="#">Quiz</a></li>
</ul>
```

Note that the second list item doesn't have the internal class added to it.

Consider the following rule:

```
nav ul li.internal:nth-of-type(n+2) a {
  color: #fe0208;
}
```

You can see that we are telling the CSS, "From the second matching item, target every <li> item with a class called internal. And here's what we see in the browser:

[

CSS3 doesn't count like jQuery!

If you're used to using jQuery you'll know that it counts from 0 upwards. For example, if selecting an element in jQuery, an integer value of 1 would actually be the second element. CSS3 however, starts at 1 so that a value of 1 is the first item it matches.
]

The negation (:not) selector

Another handy selector is the negation pseudo-class selector. This is used to select everything that isn't something else. For example, keeping the same markup as the previous example, if we change our rule as follows:

```
nav ul li:not(.internal) a {
  color: #fe0208;
}
```

You can see that we are opting to select every list item that doesn't have the internal class . So in the browser, we see this:

So far we have looked primarily at what's known as **structural pseudo-classes** (full information on this is available at `http://www.w3.org/TR/selectors/#structural-pseudos`). However, CSS3 has many more selectors. If you're working on a web application, it's worth looking at the full list of UI element states pseudo-classes (`http://www.w3.org/TR/selectors/#UIstates`), as they can; for example, help you target rules based on whether something is selected or not.

Amendments to pseudo-elements

Pseudo-elements have been around since CSS2 but the CSS3 specification revises the syntax of their use very slightly. To refresh your memory, until now, `p:first-line` would target the first line in a `<p>` tag. Or `p:first-letter` would target the first letter. Well, CSS3 asks us to separate these pseudo-elements with a double colon to differentiate them from pseudo-classes. Therefore, we should write `p::first-letter` instead. Note that however Internet Explorer 8 and lower versions don't understand the double colon syntax; they understand only the single colon syntax.

Is :first-line handy for responsive designs?

One thing that you may find particularly handy about the `:first-line` pseudo-element is that it is specific to the viewport. For example, if we write the following rule:

```
p::first-line {
  color: #ff0cff;
}
```

As you might expect, the first line is rendered in an awful shade of pink (I was thinking of Moulin Rouge at the time):

However, on a different viewport, it renders a different selection of text:

So, without needing to alter the markup, with a responsive design, there's a handy way of having the first visual (as the browser renders it, not as it appears in the markup) line of text appear differently than the others.

Hopefully this brief foray into CSS3 selectors illustrates how they help keep a responsive design and code base free of additional markup. It the past, I've needed to use a JavaScript library such as jQuery to make complicated selections but CSS3 often negates that need. It's also comforting to know that the CSS3 selectors module is already at the W3C Recommendation status; so it's a very mature module that's unlikely to change much from here on.

Custom web typography

For years we've made do with a boring selection of web safe fonts. When some fancy typography was essential for a design, we've typically substituted a graphical element for it and used a text-indent rule to shift the actual text from the viewport.

There have been a few further options for adding fancy typography to a page. sIFR (`http://www.mikeindustries.com/blog/sifr/`) and Cufón (`http://cufon.shoqolate.com/generate/`) used Flash and JavaScript respectively to re-make text elements appear as the fonts they were intended to be. However, with a responsive design, we want a lean, mean, content-serving machine, and images and code flab should be avoided where possible. Thankfully, CSS provides a means of custom web typography that is now ready for the big time.

The @font-face CSS rule

The `@font-face` CSS rule has been around since CSS2 (but subsequently absent in CSS 2.1). It was even supported partially by Internet Explorer 4 (no, really)! So what's it doing here, when we're supposed to be talking about CSS3?

Well, as it turns out, `@font-face` has been re-introduced for the CSS3 Fonts module (`http://www.w3.org/TR/css3-fonts`). Due to the historic legal quagmire of using fonts on the web, it's only recently started to gain serious traction as the de facto solution for web typography. There's also the issue of the varying font formats and implementations from different vendors. For example, the **Embedded OpenType (EOT)** font was Internet Explorer's (and not anyone else's) preferred choice of font format. Others favor the more common place **TrueType (TTF)**, whilst there is also **Scalable Vector Graphics (SVG)** and **Web Open Font Format (WOFF)**. When it comes to using `@font-face` for your web typography, there is both good news and bad. First the bad...

Until a single universal format wins out, it's necessary to serve multiple versions of the same font to cover the different browser implementations. Much as there are competing video formats, we also need a single font format for the web to emerge victorious before dropping support for the others.

However, the good news is that adding custom fonts for every browser is now easy. Let's do it!

Implementing web fonts with @font-face

Let's get the *And the winner isn't...* site typography licked into shape with the `@font-face` CSS rule.

First we need some fonts. There are now a number of great sources for web fonts; both free and paid. My personal favorite is Font Squirrel (`www.fontsquirrel.com`) although Google also offers free web fonts, ultimately served with the `@font-face` rule (`www.google.com/webfonts`). There are also great, paid services from Typekit (`www.typekit.com`) and Font Deck (`www.fontdeck.com`).

As chance would have it the fonts used in my composite are all available free from Font Squirrel (I know, I'm a cheapskate!). They are Bebas Neue, Bitstream Vera Sans and Collaborate Thin. Having downloaded the relevant `@font-face` kit for each font from Font Squirrel a look inside the ZIP file of each reveals the font itself in various formats (WOFF, TTF, EOT , and SVG) plus a `stylesheet.css` file containing a font stack for the font needed. For example, the rule for Bebas Neue is as follows:

```
@font-face {
    font-family: 'BebasNeueRegular';
    src: url('BebasNeue-webfont.eot');
    src: url('BebasNeue-webfont.eot?#iefix') format('embedded-
opentype'),
        url('BebasNeue-webfont.woff') format('woff'),
        url('BebasNeue-webfont.ttf') format('truetype'),
        url('BebasNeue-webfont.svg#BebasNeueRegular') format('svg');
    font-weight: normal;
    font-style: normal;

}
```

Much like the way vendor prefixes work, the browser will apply styles from that list of properties (with the lower properties, if applicable, taking precedence) and ignore ones it doesn't understand. That way, no matter what the browser, there should be a font that it can use.

Now, although this block of code is great for fans of copy and paste, it's important to pay attention to the paths the fonts are stored in. For example, I tend to copy the fonts from the ZIP file and store them in a folder inventively called `fonts` on the same level as my `css` folder. Therefore, as I'm usually copying this font stack rule into my main stylesheet, I need to amend the paths. So, my rule becomes:

```
@font-face {
    font-family: 'BebasNeueRegular';
    src: url('../fonts/BebasNeue-webfont.eot');
    src: url('../fonts/BebasNeue-webfont.eot?#iefix')
format('embedded-opentype'),
        url('../fonts/BebasNeue-webfont.woff') format('woff'),
        url('../fonts/BebasNeue-webfont.ttf') format('truetype'),
        url('../fonts/BebasNeue-webfont.svg#BebasNeueRegular')
format('svg');
    font-weight: normal;
    font-style: normal;

}
```

It's then just a case of setting the correct font and weight (if needed) for the relevant style rule. In this case, I want to amend the navigation links to use the new Bebas Neue font:

```
nav ul li a {
  height: 42px;
  line-height: 42px;
  text-decoration: none;
  text-transform: uppercase;
  font-family: 'BebasNeueRegular';
  font-size: 1.875em; /*30 ÷ 16 */
  color: black;
}
```

And here is how the navigation bar now looks in the browser:

When replacing fonts you'll typically need to amend the font sizing. However, having put the existing font size calculation in a comment to the side, it's easy to amend accordingly. An added bonus is that, if the composite uses the same fonts you are using in the code, you can plug the sizes in direct from the composite file. For example, my composite shows the "**EVERY YEAR...**" text as 102 px, so using the tried and trusted *target ÷ context = result* technique I can convert this value to ems:

```
#content h1 {
  font-family: Arial, Helvetica, Verdana, sans-serif;
  text-transform: uppercase;
  font-family: 'BebasNeueRegular';
  font-size: 6.375em;  /* 102 ÷ 16 */
}
```

Once I've amended the font-family and font-size declarations for all relevant rules, the front page now looks like the following in Google Chrome (using the WOFF font format):

The design still isn't perfect but the typography now perfectly mirrors that of our original composite. For comparison, here's how it's looking on the iPad 2 (which supports TTF fonts form version iOS 4.2 onwards):

Help—my CSS3 @font-face headings look messy

This problem drove me to distraction when I first started using @font-face fonts to set my web typography free. It's not particular to responsive designs, it can happen with any heading that has a @font-face font applied. Here's a portion of a design composite I was working on:

When I had built the site, the relevant markup was as follows:

```
<div class="intro">
  <h1>We're Bridestone: <span>providing <b>beautiful</b> quality
<i>natural</i> stone products.</span></h1>
  ...more code...
</div> <!-- intro:END -->
```

And here was the relevant CSS:

```
.intro h1 {
  font-family: CaudexBold, "Times New Roman", Times, serif;
  font-size: 2.63636364em;
  line-height: 1em;
}
.intro h1 span {
  font-size: 0.545454545em;
  font-family: CaudexRegular, "Times New Roman", Times, serif;
  font-weight: normal;
}
```

However, although I was using `@font-face` so that I could use exactly the same font as the composite, the header still looked a little messy in the browser:

Hopefully you can make out that the **We're Bridestone** text doesn't match the composite. It's thicker, which degrades the clarity!

It turns out that the problem relates to font weight. Unless explicitly stating the `font-weight` property, many browsers will apply a standard `font-weight` (typically, `700`) to any heading elements. The solution therefore is to always define the `font-weight` of any `@font-face` fonts used in heading elements. For example, in this instance, I amended the CSS to:

```
.productIntro h1 {
  font-family: CaudexBold, "Times New Roman", Times, serif;
  font-weight: 400;
  font-size: 2.63636364em;
  line-height: 1em;
}
```

This then overrides the `font-weight` value that the browser would ordinarily use and as shown in the following screenshot, the design finally matches the composite in the browser:

A note about custom @font-face typography and responsive designs

The `@font-face` method of web typography is, on the whole, great. The only caveats to be aware of when using the technique with responsive designs are in relation to the font file size. For example, the *And the winner isn't...* site is using three custom fonts—Bebas Neue, Bitstream Vera Sans, and Collaborate Thin. At worst, if the device rendering the page required the SVG font format, it will require an extra 70 KB of data, compared with using the standard web safe fonts such as Arial. These fonts are also fairly lightweight—others are not! Be sure to check the size of custom fonts if you want the best site performance.

A truly responsive type unit on the way?

Amongst the current working draft of the CSS3 Fonts module is reference to viewport relative fonts (`http://www.w3.org/TR/css3-values/#viewport-relative-lengths`). The **vw** unit (for viewport width), **vh** unit (for viewport height) and **vm** unit (for viewport minimum; equal to the smaller of either vm or vh) could be crucial time savers in the years to come. Sadly, at present there is no browser support apart from Internet Explorer 9.

New CSS3 color formats and alpha transparency

So far, CSS3 has given us new powers of selection and the ability to add custom typography to our designs. Now, we'll look at ways that CSS3 allows us to work with color that were simply not possible before.

Firstly, CSS3 allows us to use new methods, such as **RGB** and **HSL**, for declaring color . In addition, it enables us to use those two methods alongside an alpha channel (**RGBA** and **HSLA** respectively).

RGB color

RGB (Red, Green, and Blue) is a coloring system that's been around for decades. It works by defining different values for the red, green, and blue components of a color. For example, the red color used for the odd numbered navigation links on the *And the winner isn't...* site is currently defined in the CSS as a hex (hexadecimal) value, #fe0208:

```
nav ul li:nth-child(odd) a {
  color: #fe0208;
}
```

However, with CSS3, it can equally be described as an RGB value:

```
nav ul li:nth-child(odd) a {
  color: rgb(254, 2, 8);
}
```

Most image editing applications show colors as both hex and RGB values in their color picker. The following screenshot shows the Photoshop color picker, with the **R**, **G**, and **B** boxes showing the values for each channel:

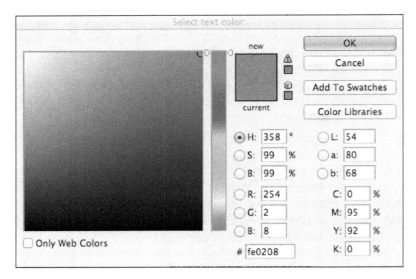

You can see that the **R** value is **254**, the **G** value is **2** and the **B** value is **8**. Which is easily transferable to the CSS color property value. In the CSS, after defining the color mode (for example, rgb) the values for red, green and blue colors are comma separated in that order within parenthesis.

HSL color

Besides RGB, CSS3 also allows us to declare color values as HSL (Hue, Saturation, and Lightness).

HSL isn't the same as HSB!

Don't make the mistake of thinking that the HSB (Hue, Saturation, and Brightness) value shown in the color picker of image editing applications such as Photoshop is the same as HSL — it isn't!

What makes HSL such a joy to use is that it's relatively simple to understand the color that will be represented based on the values given. For example, unless you're some sort of color picking Ninja, I'd wager you couldn't instantly tell me what color rgb(255, 51, 204) is? Any takers? No, me neither. However, show me the HSL value of hsl(315, 100%, 60%) and I could take a guess that it is somewhere between Magenta and Red color (it's actually a festive pink color—perhaps I'm starting to like Moulin Rouge after all). How do I know this? Simple...

HSL works on a 360° color wheel. The first figure in a HSL color, represents Hue, and has Yellow at 60°, Green at 120°, Cyan at 180°, Blue at 240°, Magenta at 300° and finally Red at 360°. So as the aforementioned HSL color had a hue of 315, it's easy to know that it will be between Magenta (at 300°) and Red (at 360°). The following two values for saturation and lightness, specified as percentages, merely alter the base hue. For a more saturated or colorful appearance, use a higher percentage in the second value. The final value, controlling the lightness, can vary between 0 percent for black and 100 percent for white.

So, once you've defined a color as an HSL value, it's also easy to create variations on it, merely by altering the saturation and lightness percentages. For example, our red navigation links can be defined in HSL values as follows:

```
nav ul li:nth-child(odd) a {
  color: hsl(359, 99%, 50%);
}
```

If we wanted to make a slightly darker color on hover, we could use the same HSL value and merely alter the lightness (the final value) percentage value only, as shown in the following code snippet:

```
nav ul li:nth-child(odd) a:hover {
  color: hsl(359, 99%, 40%);
}
```

In conclusion, if you can remember the mnemonic Young Guys Can Be Messy Rascals (or any other mnemonic you care to memorize) for the HSL color wheel, you'll be able to approximately write HSL color values without resorting to a color picker and also create variations upon it. Show that trick to the savant backend PHP and .NET guys at the office party and earn some quick kudos!

Fallback color values for IE6, IE7, and IE8

As you might have guessed, RGB and HSL are not supported in Internet Explorer versions below IE9. Therefore, if a fallback color declaration is needed for these browsers, specify it first before the RGB or HSL value. For example, the navigation link rule defined above could have a hex fallback specified like this:

```
nav ul li:nth-child(odd) a {
  color: #fe0208;
  color: hsl(359, 99%, 50%);
}
```

Alpha channels

So far you'd be forgiven for wondering why on earth we'd bother using HSL or RGB instead of our trusty hex values we've been using for years. Where HSL and RGB differ from hex is that they allow the use of an alpha transparency channel. This means one element with an alpha transparency will show what's beneath it.

Let's make some amendments to the *And the winner isn't...* home page to illustrate. First, we'll set a grungy background image in the body element, as follows:

```
body {
  background: url(../img/grunge.jpg) repeat;
}
```

Now, we'll add a white background in the #wrapper div (which encloses all the other elements). However, instead of setting a solid white color with a hex value, we'll set a HSLA value as shown in the highlighted line in the following code snippet:

```
#wrapper {
  margin-right: auto;
  margin-left: auto;
  width: 96%; /* Holding outermost DIV */
  max-width: 1414px;
  background-color: hsla(0, 0%, 100%, 0.8);
}
```

An HSLA color declaration is similar in syntax to a standard HSL rule. However, in addition, you must declare the value as hsla (rather than merely hsl) and add an additional opacity value, given as a decimal value between 0 (completely transparent) and 1 (completely opaque). Here, we have specified that our white #wrapper isn't completely opaque. The following screenshot shows how it looks in the browser:

The RGBA syntax follows the same convention as the HSLA equivalent, using an additional opacity value after the color:

```
background-color: rgba(255, 255, 255, 0.8);
```

Hopefully you can see that the addition of an alpha channel to both the RGB and HSL color modes, allows us a great deal of flexibility when layering elements. It means that we no longer have to rely on the transparency of images (PNG and GIF images, for example) to achieve this type of visual effect, which is great news when building a responsive design.

Why not just use opacity?

CSS3 also allows elements to have opacity set with the opacity declaration. A value is set between zero and one in decimal increments (for example, opacity set to 0.1 is 10 percent). However, this differs from RGBA and HSLA in that setting an opacity value on an element affects the entire element. Whereas, setting a value with HSLA or RGBA meanwhile allows particular parts of an element to have an alpha layer. For example, an element could have an HSLA value for the background but a solid color for the text within it.

The CSS3 Color module was the first of the CSS3 modules to reach the advanced Recommendation stage. Therefore, like the CSS3 Selectors module, CSS3 Colors are good to use right away, safe in the knowledge that the method of implementation is unlikely to change from this point onwards.

Summary

In this chapter, we've learned how to easily select almost anything we need on the page with CSS3's new selectors. We've also looked at how we can make responsive columns for content in record time and solve common and annoying problems such as long URL wrapping. We now also have an understanding of CSS3's new color module and how we can apply colors with RGB and HSL complete with transparent alpha layers for great aesthetic effects. In this chapter, we've also learned how to add custom fonts to a design with the @font-face rule, finally freeing us from the shackles of the humdrum selection of "web-safe" fonts we're used to designing with. Despite all these great new features and techniques, we've only picked at the surface of what we can do with CSS3. Let's move on now and look at even more ways CSS3 can make a responsive design as fast, efficient, and maintainable as possible with CSS3 text shadows, box shadows, gradients, and multiple backgrounds.

6
Stunning Aesthetics
with CSS3

In the previous chapter we learned about some quick and useful CSS3 techniques to aid in building responsive designs. We also made a big difference to the visuals by employing the CSS3 @font-face rule to apply custom typography and learned about CSS3's tools for selecting DOM elements. So, with some CSS3 basics covered, let's look at some more advanced features of CSS3; how we can give a responsive design an aesthetic lift by using some of the more exciting CSS3 techniques that, for the vast majority, don't require a single graphics image, making our responsive design as bandwidth friendly as possible.

In this chapter we will cover:

- How to create text-shadows with CSS3
- How to create box-shadows (drop shadows) with CSS3
- Making gradient backgrounds with CSS3
- Using multiple backgrounds with CSS3
- Using CSS3 background gradients to make patterns
- Using the CSS3 @font-face rule to make bandwidth friendly icons

At this point I'm going to reiterate why I believe CSS3 is so useful in responsive design: using CSS3, rather than images in a bandwidth design reduces http requests (and hence makes the pages load faster) and makes the design more flexible and maintainable. Those benefits would be useful even on a typical fixed-width 'desktop' design but it's even more important with a responsive design as it easily allows different size box or text shadows at different viewports—without needing to make and export a single image. I'm presuming you're with me on this, so let's dig in.

Vendor prefixes

When implementing CSS3, just remember to add relevant vendor prefixes to ensure the broadest cross-browser compatibility. Alternately, if you're happy to add some JavaScript to your code, consider the afore mentioned **-prefix-free** script. It automatically adds relevant vendor prefixes to any CSS3 rules that need them, allowing you to only write the W3C version in your stylesheet. Get it here: `http://leaverou.github.com/prefixfree/`.

Text shadows with CSS3

One of the most widely implemented CSS3 features is 'text-shadow'. Like `@font-face`, it had a previous life but was dropped in CSS 2.1. Thankfully it's back and widely supported (all modern browsers and Internet Explorer 9 onwards).

Let's look at the basic syntax:

```
.element {
    text-shadow: 1px 1px 1px #cccccc;
}
```

Remember, the values in shorthand rules always go right and then down. Therefore, the first value is the amount of shadow to the right, the second is the amount down, the third value is the amount of blur (the distance the shadow travels before fading to nothing), and the final value is the color.

HEX, HSL, or RGB color allowed

The color value doesn't need to be defined as a HEX value. It can just as easily be HSL(A) or RGB(A) :

```
text-shadow: 4px 4px 0px hsla(140, 3%, 26%, 0.4);
```

However, keep in mind that the browser must then also support HSL/RGB color modes along with `text-shadow` in order to render the effect. If I'd really like to use HSLA or RGBA (because of the opacity capability) I tend to do this:

```
text-shadow: 4px 4px 0px #404442;
text-shadow: 4px 4px 0px hsla(140, 3%, 26%, 0.4);
```

Define the shadow first with a HEX value (as a fall back for older browsers) and then repeat the rule afterwards using the HSLA or RGBA value.

Pixels, em, or rem

You can also set the shadow values in em or rem. For example, here's the **AND THE WINNER ISN'T** composite:

In Photoshop, the **EVERY YEAR** text is 102 px with a text shadow of 4 px. Therefore, using the trusty **target ÷ context = result** formula (4 ÷ 102 = .039215686). So this becomes:

```
text-shadow: .039215686em .039215686em 0em #dad7d7; /* 4 ÷ 102 */
```

The following screenshot shows the effect in the browser:

Personally, I rarely use em or rem for text-shadow values. As the values are always really low, using 1 or 2 px generally looks good across all viewports.

Preventing a text shadow

Depending on your eyesight, you *may* notice that we now also have a text shadow on the second sentence, **WHEN I WATCH THE OSCARS I'M ANNOYED...**. Here's why:

```
<h1>Every year <em>when I watch the Oscars I'm annoyed...</em></h1>
```

The text-shadow is currently applying to the entire `<h1>` tag (which includes the `<em>` tag within it) so we need to remove the `text-shadow` from the `<em>` tag:

```
#content h1 em {
    font-family: 'BitstreamVeraSansRoman';
    display: block;
    line-height: 1.052631579em; /* 40 ÷ 38 */
    color: #757474;
    font-size: .352941176em; /* 36 ÷ 102 */
    text-shadow: none;
}
```

And now it's looking good:

Left and top shadows

Shadows to the left and above can be achieved using negative values. For example:

```
text-shadow: -4px -4px 0px #dad7d7;
```

Adds an effect like the following:

If there is no blur to be added to a `text-shadow` the value can be omitted from the declaration, for example:

```
text-shadow: -4px -4px #dad7d7;
```

The spec assumes that the first two values are for the offsets if no third value is declared.

Creating an embossed text-shadow effect

I've always felt that `text-shadow` works best for creating embossed text. This effect usually works best with a highlight color (for example, white or close to it) applied to dark text on a non-white background. Let's add an embossed effect to the navigation links:

```
nav ul li a {
    height: 42px;
    line-height: 42px;
    text-decoration: none;
    text-transform: uppercase;
    font-family: 'BebasNeueRegular';
    font-size: 1.875em; /*30 ÷ 16 */
    color: #000000;
    text-shadow: 0 1px 0 hsla(0, 0%, 100%, 0.75);
}
```

And here's the result. Subtle but effective—just a little depth added without shouting LOOK AT MY TEXT-SHADOW!

For the best embossed text, I tend to find that 1 or 2 px in the vertical offset and nothing for blur and horizontal offset works best.

Multiple text-shadows

It's possible to add multiple text shadows by comma separating two values. For example:

```
text-shadow: 0px 1px #ffffff,4px 4px 0px #dad7d7;
```

As ever, subtlety is necessary or type can become illegible. I'm going to use this declaration to combine both the previous embossed effect and the existing text-shadow. Here's the effect in the browser:

Read the W3C specification for the `text-shadow` property here: `http://www.w3.org/TR/css3-text/#text-shadow`

Box shadows

Once text-shadows are understood, box-shadows will be a piece of cake. Principally, they follow exactly the same syntax: horizontal offset, vertical offset, blur, and color:

```
box-shadow: 0px 3px 5px #444444;
```

However, they aren't as well supported across browsers so it's wise to use vendor prefixes to maximize compatibility. For example:

```
-ms-box-shadow: 0px 3px 5px #444444;
-moz-box-shadow: 0px 3px 5px #444444;
-webkit-box-shadow: 0px 3px 5px #444444;
box-shadow: 0px 3px 5px #444444;
```

We'll use this to add a box shadow to the film posters in the sidebar of the **AND THE WINNER ISN'T** site:

```
.sideBlock img {
    max-width: 45%;
    box-shadow: 0px 3px 5px #444444;
}
```

Here's the effect in the browser:

Inset shadow

The box-shadow property can also be used to create an inset shadow — this applies within the targeted element, as opposed to the outside, as a normal box shadow would. It's useful for creating vignette effects for example. Here is the syntax:

```
box-shadow:inset 0 0 40px #000000;
```

Everything functions as before but the inset part of the declaration instructs the browser to set the effect on the **inside**. I'm going to use this rule now on the <body> tag to create a vignette effect for the entire page. The idea is make a shadow appear from all the edges of our page.

```
body {
    -moz-box-shadow:inset 0 0 30px #000000;
    -webkit-box-shadow:inset 0 0 30px #000000;
    box-shadow:inset 0 0 30px #000000;
}
```

Here's what the effect looks like in the browser:

Multiple shadows

Like text-shadows, you can have multiple box-shadows. Again, merely separate the values with a comma and they are applied top to bottom as they are listed. I remind myself of the order by thinking that the declaration nearest to the top in the rule (in the code) appears nearest to the 'top' of the order when displayed in the browser.

```
box-shadow: inset 0 0 30px hsl(0, 0%, 0%),
            inset 0 0 70px hsla(0, 97%, 53%, 1);
```

I've added this to my body rule and it produces an awful red boudoir effect. Must be the by-product of having an image of Moulin Rouge on the page!

Suffice to say, I'm taking that declaration straight out! However, this demonstrates the power of using CSS3 to toy with design ideas. Adding visual flourishes and removing them is a matter of seconds without having to touch a graphics editor.

 You can read the W3C specification for the `box-shadow` property here: `http://www.w3.org/TR/css3-background/#the-box-shadow`

Background gradients

When not using CSS3, if we want an element to have some sort of background gradient, we use a thin graphical slice and then tile it horizontally/vertically. As graphics resources go, it's quite an economical tradeoff. An image, only a pixel or two wide, isn't going to break the bandwidth bank and on a single site it can be used on multiple elements.

Linear background gradients

Let's start with this technique to make a linear background gradient for the sidebar of the **AND THE WINNER ISN'T** site:

```
aside {
    border-right-color: #e8e8e8;
    border-right-style: solid;
    border-right-width: 2px;
    margin-top: 58px;
    padding-left: 1.5%;
    padding-right: 1.0416667%;
    margin-left: 1.0416667%;
    float: left;
    width: 20.7083333%;
    background: url(../img/sidebarBg2.png) 50% repeat-x;
}
```

Here's how it looks in a browser:

However, it still requires trips to the graphics editor when we want to amend the effect. Plus occasionally, content can 'break out' of the gradient background, extending beyond its fixed size limitations. This problem is compounded with a responsive design, as we want the page structure to have the ability to change shape (for example, getting longer or wider) significantly without breaking up the design.

For example, let's suppose I wanted to add another two films in each section. Here's what happens:

It's not terrible but the grey gradient certainly isn't spanning the whole sidebar section, as I'd like. Ordinarily, I'd have to head back to my graphics editor and re-make the graphic. With a CSS3 gradient however, things are far more flexible. Here's the syntax for the same gradient in pure CSS3, instead of using an image:

```
background: linear-gradient(90deg, #ffffff 0%, #e4e4e4 50%,
                            #ffffff 100%);
```

And here's how it looks in a supporting browser:

No matter how long that section gets (after all, there are plenty of films I could enthuse and moan about in equal measure), the CSS3 gradient will always cover the area.

The only significant fly in the ointment of background gradient nirvana is that they aren't supported as well as some of the other CSS3 features. Internet Explorer 9 doesn't have native support for them for instance (although it is promised for Internet Explorer 10). However, background gradients are supported in most other browsers, albeit with vendor prefixes. It shouldn't stop you from using them to enhance designs for browsers that support them now and others that will in the near future. As a fallback for older browsers, it's sometimes preferable to define a solid background color first so that older browsers at least render a solid background if they don't understand the gradient rules.

Note: there used to be different background gradient syntaxes

Historically, there were a number of different syntaxes employed by different browser vendors to render the same background gradient effect. Webkit was the main offender but thankfully, since Safari 5.1 they have adopted the same conventions as Mozilla — the conventions that the W3C is also using.

Breakdown of linear gradient syntax

The linear background gradient syntax (refer to the following example) is potentially confusing so let's break it down:

- Within the parenthesis the first (optional) value (in this case `90deg`) defines the direction the gradient starts off in. Leaving this out defaults to a vertical top to bottom gradient. You can also use values like `to top right`, which would be a diagonal gradient ending at the top right.

- The next value (`#ffffff 0%` in this example) is the 'starting point' — a color value given as the color and then the position. You could also use something like `blue 20%` which would then start fading from blue to the next color at 20 percent along the imaginary line from beginning to end of the linear gradient. Equally, you could set a negative value for the position so that the gradient begins before it is actually visible. For example:

```
background: linear-gradient(90deg, #ffffff -50%, #e4e4e4 50%,
                            #ffffff 100%);
```

This line means that the gradient would start 50 percent before the beginning of the visible area the imaginary line travels along.

- The next value is a 'color stop'. Let's recap where we're at: in our example we are moving in an upwards direction at 90 degrees (`90deg`), starting with white (`#ffffff 0%`), and moving towards a color value of `#e4e4e4` (a light grey color) at 50 percent along the line. This is our first 'color stop' within the gradient. We can use multiple color stops if we like, (separated by commas) before we define our 'ending point'.

- The final value in parenthesis (`#ffffff 100%` in our example) is always the 'ending point' of the gradient. Regardless of how many color stops are placed after the starting point, the final value is always the ending point.

> Read the W3C specification for linear background gradients at:
> `http://dev.w3.org/csswg/css3-images/#linear-gradients`

Radial background gradients

CSS3 background gradients aren't limited to linear gradients. It's equally simple to create a radial gradient. These begin from a central point and spread out smoothly in an elliptical or circular shape.

Here's the syntax for a radial background gradient:

```
background: radial-gradient(center, ellipse cover, #ffffff 72%,
                            #dddddd 100%);
```

Adding this declaration to our `#content` rule results in the following effect:

See that subtle darkening at the corners? That's our radial gradient. Let's break the syntax down to see what's going on.

Breakdown of radial gradient syntax

After specifying the property (`background:`) we specify that we'd like a `radial-gradient` (rather than a linear one). Then, within parenthesis we specify the starting point. In the previous example, we used `center` but we could equally use something like `25px 25px` to start 25 px from the top and left of the element. For example:

```
background: radial-gradient(25px 25px, ellipse cover, #ffffff 72%,
                           #dddddd 100%);
```

This line of code produces the following effect:

The center is 25 px from the top left of the element and then radiates smoothly outwards.

The next value in our declaration is more straightforward; it's the shape and size the radial gradient should take:

```
background: radial-gradient(center, ellipse cover, #ffffff 72%,
                           #dddddd 100%);
```

For shape, the options are either `circle` (the gradient will radiate uniformly in all directions) or `ellipse` (which will radiate different amounts in different directions). However, there's quite a bit of flexibility in how the shape is sized. The size can be any of the following:

- `closest-side`: the shape meets the side of the box nearest to the center (in the case of circles), or meets both the horizontal and vertical sides that are closest to the center (in the case of ellipses)

- `closest-corner`: the shape meets exactly the closest corner of the box from its center

- `farthest-side`: the opposite of `closest-side`, in that rather than the shape meeting the nearest size, it's sized to meet the one farthest from its center (or both the furthest vertical and horizontal side in the case of an ellipse)

- `farthest-corner`: the shape expands to the farthest corner of the box from the center

- `cover`: identical to `farthest-corner`

- `contain`: identical to `closest-side`

It's then a matter of defining the starting point, color stops, and end point (in exactly the same manner as linear gradients).

For example, if we changed our rule to this:

```
background: radial-gradient(20px 20px, circle cover,
                        hsla(9,69%,85%,0.5) 0%,
                        hsla(9,76%,63%,1) 50%,
                        hsla(10,98%,46%,1) 51%,
                        hsla(24,100%,50%,1) 75%,
                        hsla(10,100%,39%,1) 100%);
```

You can see we are starting 20 pixels from the left and top, using a circle to cover the area and using multiple HSL(A) color stops. Here's how it looks:

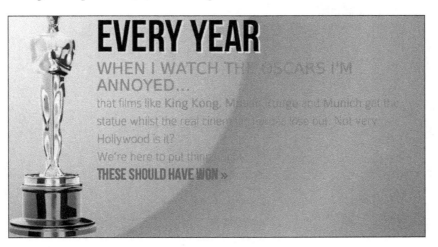

Hopefully, while this isn't the best lesson in aesthetics, it demonstrates the power of using pure CSS3 to achieve visual effects.

 Read the W3C specification for radial background gradients at: `http://dev.w3.org/csswg/css3-images/#radial-gradients`

The cheat's way to perfect CSS3 linear and radial gradients

If writing out a CSS3 gradient seems like hard work there are some great online gradient generators. My personal favorite is http://www.colorzilla.com/gradient-editor/. It uses a graphics editor style GUI, allowing you to pick your colors, stops, gradient style (linear and radial gradients are supported), and even the color space (HEX, RGB(A), HSL(A)) you'd like the final gradient in. There are also loads of preset gradients to use as starting points. If that wasn't enough, it even gives you optional code for fixing up Internet Explorer 9 to show the gradient and a fallback flat color for older browsers. Still not convinced? How about the ability to generate a gradient based on an existing image? Thought that might swing it for you.

Repeating gradients

CSS3 also gives us the ability to create repeating background gradients. Let's take a look at how it's done:

```
background: repeating-linear-gradient(90deg, #ffffff 0px,
            hsla(0, 1%, 50%,0.1) 5px);
```

And here's how that looks applied to the sidebar:

Firstly, prefix the `linear-gradient` or `radial-gradient` with 'repeating', then it follows the same syntax as a normal gradient. Here I've used pixel distances between the white and grey colors (`0px` and `5px` respectively) but you could also choose to use percentages. For best results, it's recommended to stick to the same measurement units (such as, pixels or percentages) within a gradient.

Let's try a repeating radial gradient:

```
background: repeating-radial-gradient(2px 2px, ellipse,
         hsla(0,0%,100%,1) 2px, hsla(0,0%,95%,1) 10px,
         hsla(0,0%,93%,1) 15px, hsla(0,0%,100%,1) 20px);
```

It's very similar to the standard radial gradient used earlier. I've merely amended the start point, removed the 'cover' value as it's not needed and then set distances for each color stop in pixels. My end point is `20px` so the pattern repeats every 20 pixels. Here's that rule applied to the `body`. I'll warn you now—it isn't pretty!

Read the W3C information on repeating gradients at: `http://dev.` `w3.org/csswg/css3-images/#repeating-gradients`

There's one more way of using background gradients I'd like to share with you.

Background gradient patterns

It no doubt depends on your own design sensibilities but although I've often used subtle linear gradients in designs I've found less practical use for radial gradients and repeating gradients. However, clever folks out there have harnessed all these background techniques together to create background gradient patterns. Let's look at an example. Instead of the repeating radial gradient I just added to the `body`, I'll add this:

```
body {
    background-color:white;
    background-image:
      radial-gradient(hsla(0, 0%, 87%, 0.31) 9px, transparent 10px),
      repeating-radial-gradient(hsla(0, 0%, 87%, 0.31) 0,
                hsla(0, 0%, 87%, 0.31) 4px, transparent 5px,
                transparent 20px, hsla(0, 0%, 87%, 0.31) 21px,
                hsla(0, 0%, 87%, 0.31) 25px, transparent 26px,
                transparent 50px);
    background-size: 30px 30px, 90px 90px;
    background-position: 0 0;
}
```

Here's what that gives me in the browser:

How about that? Just a few lines of CSS3 and we have an easily editable, scalable background pattern by using the background gradient techniques we've already looked at.

CSS Ninja, Lea Verou has collated a growing resource of CSS3 background patterns, available at `http://lea.verou.me/css3patterns/`.

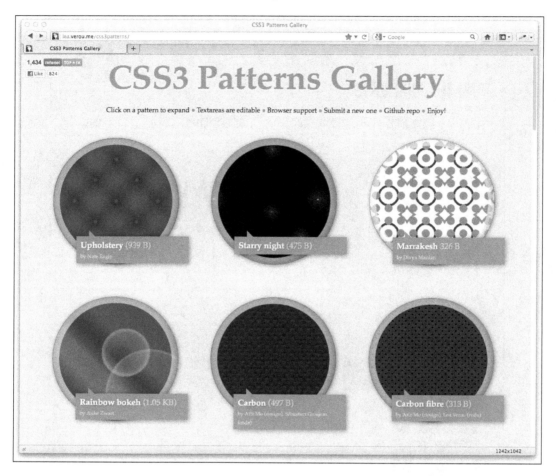

Responsive considerations for CSS3

It's worth remembering that different declarations can be used for different viewports. For example, although I might not mind the way the gradient pattern looks on smaller viewports:

I may choose not to use it for larger viewports (for example 768 px wide and greater). I can therefore just create a specific rule for the background gradient using media queries:

```
@media screen and (max-width: 768px) {
  body {
    background-color:white;
    background-image:
      radial-gradient(hsla(0, 0%, 87%, 0.31) 9px, transparent 10px),
```

```
        repeating-radial-gradient(hsla(0, 0%, 87%, 0.31) 0,
        hsla(0, 0%, 87%, 0.31) 4px, transparent 5px, transparent 20px,
        hsla(0, 0%, 87%, 0.31) 21px, hsla(0, 0%, 87%, 0.31) 25px,
        transparent 26px, transparent 50px);
    background-size: 30px 30px, 90px 90px;
    background-position: 0 0;
  }
}
```

Remember that media queries will allow you to specify every element differently for different viewports if you wish. It's all about presenting the best experience.

Writing CSS3 easily with CSS pre-processors

CSS3 rules currently require multiple vendor prefix properties. An alternative to storing clippings of these prefixes for every declaration, or using a JavaScript file to add prefixes in the browser are CSS pre-processors like SASS and LESS. For example, using SASS with the Compass plugin allows you to write a simple box shadow rule like this: `element { @include box-shadow; }`. When the CSS is generated, it includes a full stack of vendor specific rules along with the relevant Internet Explorer hacks (if available). If this wasn't a big enough reason to take a look, consider that pre-processors also add the ability to use variables and programming conventions like `if`/`while` statements. Find out more about SASS at `http://sass-lang.com` and LESS at `http://lesscss.org`

Bringing CSS3 properties together

Until now, we've largely been looking at abstract implementations of various CSS3 features. Let's use them together now to create our **THESE SHOULD HAVE WON>>** link. On the original Photoshop composite file for the **AND THE WINNER ISN'T** website, the button text uses custom typography, which we've already dealt with in *Chapter 5, CSS3: Selectors, Typography, and Color Modes*. However, it also has a red gradient background with rounded corners and a drop shadow behind it. This is what we have defined in the stylesheet currently:

```
#content a {
    text-decoration: none;
    font: 2.25em /* 36px ÷ 16 */ 'BebasNeueRegular';
}
```

First, let's add a solid background color for older browsers. That way, should they be unable to render the gradient, they will at least get a solid red background. I've purposely used a HEX value here because if the older browser doesn't understand gradients, it's unlikely to support RGB and HSL color modes:

```
#content a {
    text-decoration: none;
    font: 2.25em /* 36px ÷ 16 */ 'BebasNeueRegular';
    background-color: #b01c20;
}
```

Next, let's add our rounded corners. Note that, as in the rest of this chapter, for all the CSS3 properties I'll be adding it may be necessary to define vendor prefixes. I have omitted them here for the sake of brevity:

```
#content a {
    text-decoration: none;
    font: 2.25em /* 36px ÷ 16 */ 'BebasNeueRegular';
    background-color: #b01c20;
    border-radius: 8px;
}
```

Here's what we've got at this point:

Now, let's make the text white (again, as I want this viewable on older browsers, I've stuck to a simple color definition) and add padding (you could use percentage based padding too) so there's always a little space around the text:

```
#content a {
    text-decoration: none;
    font: 2.25em /* 36px ÷ 16 */ 'BebasNeueRegular';
    background-color: #b01c20;
    border-radius: 8px;
    color: white;
    padding: 30px;
}
```

Here's what that gives us:

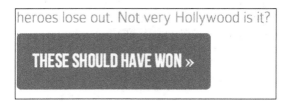

At this point the padding is encroaching on the text above so we'll add a `float:` `left` declaration along with the gradient:

```
#content a {
    text-decoration: none;
    font: 2.25em /* 36px ÷ 16 */ 'BebasNeueRegular';
    background-color: #b01c20;
    border-radius: 8px;
    color: white;
    padding: 30px;
    float: left;
    background: linear-gradient(90deg, #b01c20 0%, #f15c60 100%);
}
```

Now it's starting to take shape in the browser:

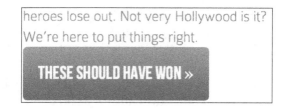

Besides adding a little margin above, I'll also go ahead and add the box shadow:

```
#content a {
    text-decoration: none;
    font: 2.25em /* 36px ÷ 16 */ 'BebasNeueRegular';
    background-color: #b01c20;
    border-radius: 8px;
    color: white;
    padding: 30px;
    float: left;
    background: -moz-linear-gradient(90deg, #b01c20 0%,
                                     #f15c60 100%);
    margin-top: 30px;
    box-shadow: 5px 5px 5px hsla(0, 0%, 26.6667%, 0.8);
}
```

And a quick check in the browser reveals we're almost done:

Now, although it's not in the Photoshop file, I'm going to add a little `text-shadow` and a thin white border, just to give it a slightly embossed feel. That's the beauty of using CSS rather than image files — it's easy to evaluate changes on the fly!

```
#content a {
    text-decoration: none;
    font: 2.25em /* 36px ÷ 16 */ 'BebasNeueRegular';
    background-color: #b01c20;
    border-radius: 8px;
    color: white;
    padding: 30px;
    float: left;
    background: -moz-linear-gradient(90deg, #b01c20 0%,
                                    #f15c60 100%);
    margin-top: 30px;
    box-shadow: 5px 5px 5px hsla(0, 0%, 26.6667%, 0.8);
    text-shadow: 0px 1px black;
    border: 1px solid #bfbfbf;
}
```

Now here's how our button looks in Firefox 8:

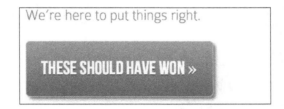

The only issue left is that our double angle quotes symbol (`&raquo;` in HTML) in the Photoshop file is in a different font from the main text. I don't feel that loading an extra font for the single character is worthwhile in this instance, so I'm going to wrap that symbol in an inline tag so that I can increase the size. Here's the amended markup:

```
<a href="#">these should have won <span>&raquo;</span></a>
```

Additionally, here's the extra CSS rule to adjust the size:

```
#content a span {
    font-size: 1.3em;
}
```

Which finishes things off nicely:

What's great about this as CSS3, rather than an image, is that it can contain whatever content is needed, and it will never break up:

Multiple background images

A common design requirement is to build a page with a different background image at the top of the page than at the bottom. Or perhaps different images for the top and bottom of a content section within a page. It seems such a straightforward requirement, that it's understandable to assume this could be easily achieved with CSS. However, with CSS2.1, achieving the effect typically required additional markup. For example, until CSS3, this is how I've always solved the problem:

```
<body class="headerBackgroundHere">

<div class="footerBackground">
  <div id="container">
    <header>
      // Header content here
    </header>
    <div id="main" role="main">
      // Main content here
    </div>
    <footer>
      // Footer content here
    </footer>
  </div>

</div> <!--! end of .footerBackground -->

</body>
```

You'll notice the entire content container (which is the `div` with an `id` of `container`) is wrapped in a `div` with the class `footerBackground`. With this in place we can target a CSS rule to set the background image for the top of the page on the `body` tag:

```
body {
    background-image: url("../img/topSlice.png");
    background-repeat: repeat-x;
}
```

Then another rule for `footerBackground`. This is where we'll place the image we want for the bottom of the page.

```
.footerBackground {
    background-image: url("../img/bottomSlice.png");
    background-repeat: repeat-x;
    background-position: bottom;
}
```

This technique works well and consistently across most browsers. However, I'm never a fan of adding additional markup merely to solve presentational problems.

Thankfully this problem is easily solved with the CSS3 as it allows multiple backgrounds for an element (part of the **CSS Backgrounds and Borders Module Level 3**). It's well supported, with Internet Explorer 8 and below being the only notable exceptions. Here's the syntax:

```
background:
    url('../img/1.png'),
    url('../img/2.png'),
    url('../img/3.png');
```

As with the stacking order of multiple shadows, the image listed first appears nearest to the 'top' in the browser. You can also add a general color for the background in the same declaration if you wish, like this:

```
background:
    url('../img/1.png'),
    url('../img/2.png'),
    url('../img/3.png') left bottom, black;
```

Specify the color last and this will show below every image specified above.

Browsers that don't understand the multiple backgrounds rule (such as Internet Explorer 8 and below) will ignore the rule altogether so you may wish to declare a 'normal' background property immediately before a CSS3 multiple background rule as a fallback for older browsers.

With the multiple backgrounds, as long as you're using PNG files with transparency, any partially transparent background images that sit on top of another will show through below. However, background images don't have to sit on top of one another, nor do they all have to be the same size.

Background size

To set different sizes for each image, use the `background-size` property. When multiple images have been used, the syntax works like this:

```
background-size: 100% 50%, 300px 400px, auto;
```

The size values (first width, then height) for each image are declared, separated by commas in the order they are listed in the background property. As in the example above, you can use percentage or pixel values for each image alongside the following:

- `auto`: which sets the element at its native size
- `cover`: which expands the image, preserving its aspect ratio, to cover the area of the element

- `contain`: which expands the image to fit its longest side within the element while preserving the aspect ratio

Background position

Another thing that's possible is to specify different positions for the different images. We could do that by amending the rule like this:

```
background:
    url('../img/1.png') center,
    url('../img/2.png'),
    url('../img/3.png') left bottom, black;
```

Where no position is declared, as in the second image, the default position of top left is used.

Background shorthand

There is a shorthand method of combining the different background properties together. However, my experience so far has been that it produces erratic results. Therefore, I tend to use the longhand method and declare the multiple images first, then the size, and then the position.

Read the W3C documentation on multiple background elements here: `http://www.w3.org/TR/css3-background/#layering`

Read about background sizing here: `http://www.w3.org/TR/css3-background/#the-background-size`

And background positions here: `http://www.w3.org/TR/css3-background/#the-background-position`

More CSS3 features

We've by no means covered all the goodies CSS3 has to offer. However, these are the ones that seem to be finding most traction in the real world. They are also the techniques I feel most benefit generating visual effects economically and flexibly for responsive designs. However, as always, keep an eye on the various CSS3 modules as there's sure to be something that will ignite your interest beyond the slice we've covered here.

Sizeable icons which are perfect for responsive designs

Smart people are already extending what's possible with CSS3 to great effect. One technique I've seen implemented that I love and now use regularly myself is using `@font-face` icons in a design.

"What are they?" I hear you cry. Well, my inquisitive friend, I'll tell you. Remember we used the CSS3 `@font-face` rules in the previous chapter to apply custom typography to our design? `@font-face` icons are merely fonts specifically made to create commonly used icons. Instead of using lots of separate graphics files for each icon, or even grouping them together into a single, larger sprite image, `@font-face` icons allow you to apply a single font for every included icon (that's just one `http` request — woo hoo!). What's more, as it's a font, it scales beautifully — perfect for responsive designs. Fico is a great example, check it out here: `http://fico.lensco.be/`.

Summary

In this chapter we've used a broader selection of CSS3's new features. CSS3's background gradients have enabled us to create some great looking background effects with pure code. We even used them to create background patterns. We've also learned how to use `text-shadows` to create an embossed effect on text and `box-shadows` to add drop-shadow effects to the outside and inside of elements.

When designing responsively, creating these aesthetic effects with pure CSS3 is a huge bonus; it means elements will not break out of any constraints usually associated with more resource heavy and inflexible images. That said, there are times when the use of images is unavoidable. But CSS3 gives us greater flexibility here too. For example, in this chapter we used CSS3's multiple background images feature to add multiple backgrounds and position them independently on the page; a technique that negates the need for extra markup, as has historically always been required. And remember, we're mostly using these effects to add visual flourishes to our responsive design, the kind of subtleties and niceties that modern browsers, regardless of their viewport size, can enjoy. Whilst tiring older browsers like Internet Explorer can't render them, they equally do them no harm.

So far however, all our forays into CSS3 have been static; elements that sit in place and remain stationary on the page in one state or another. However, CSS3 can do much more. In the next chapter we'll look at ways to transition from one state to another and take our CSS where it's never gone before: the domain of animation.

7
CSS3 Transitions, Transformations, and Animations

In the last two chapters we looked at some of the new features and functionality that CSS3 provides. However, until now, everything we have looked at has been static. But CSS3 can do more.

At present, chances are, if you need to animate elements on a web page you'll either write your own JavaScript to perform the required action or turn to a popular JavaScript library like jQuery to do the heavy lifting. However, someone involved with CSS3 clearly has issues with JavaScript's ubiquity in this area and they're looking to encroach on JavaScript's dominance. While CSS3 isn't likely to usurp jQuery or the like anytime soon, it's perfectly capable of things like smoothing transitions (for example, on mouse hover) and moving elements around the screen. This is great news for us, as it means for the growing number of devices sporting modern browsers (recent smart phones for example), we can use CSS to provide animations rather than relying on JavaScript. The upshot: you can probably scratch 'learn how to animate elements with jQuery' off the 'to do' list as we can now do all that fun stuff in pure CSS. As ever, these CSS3 features don't break anything for browsers lacking the features; they'll just skip over the rules they don't understand like they weren't there.

In this chapter, we'll cover:

- What CSS3 transitions are and how we can use them
- How to write a CSS3 transition and its shorthand syntax
- CSS3 transition timing functions (ease, cubic-bezier, and so on)

- Fun transitions for responsive web sites
- What CSS3 transformations are and how we can use them
- Understanding different 2D transformations (scale, rotate, skew, translate, and so on)
- Dabbling with 3D transformations
- Animating with CSS3 (using keyframes)

What CSS3 transitions are and how we can use them

When styling hyperlinks in CSS, it's common practice to create a hover state; an obvious way to make users aware that the item they are hovering over is a link. They're of less relevance to the growing number of touch screen devices but for everyone else, they're a great and simple interaction between website and user.

Traditionally, using only CSS, hover states are an on/off affair. There is one state as the default, that instantly changes to a different state on hover. However, CSS3 transitions, as the name implies, allow us to transition between one state and another. It's not specific to hover states but let's start there.

In the previous chapter, we created a CSS3 button with a red gradient background. This is the CSS3 used (with the additional vendor prefixes removed for brevity):

```
#content a {
    text-decoration: none;
    font: 2.25em /* 36px ÷ 16 */ 'BebasNeueRegular';
    background-color: #b01c20;
    border-radius: 8px;
    color: #ffffff;
    padding: 3%;
    float: left;
    background: linear-gradient(90deg, #b01c20 0%, #f15c60 100%);
    margin-top: 30px;
    box-shadow: 5px 5px 5px hsla(0, 0%, 26.6667%, 0.8);
    text-shadow: 0px 1px black;
    border: 1px solid #bfbfbf;
}
```

Let's add a hover state:

```
#content a:hover {
    border: 1px solid #000000;
    color: #000000;
    text-shadow: 0px 1px white;
}
```

And here are the two states, first the default:

And then here's the hover state:

It's a simple change of text, text-shadow, and border color on hover. So, as you might imagine, with the current CSS, hovering the mouse over snaps from the first state (white text) button to the second (black text); it's an on/off affair. Let's add a little CSS3 magic to our first rule:

```
#content a {
    /*…existing styles…*/
    transition: all 1s ease 0s;
}
```

Now when we hover over the button, the text, text-shadow, and border color all transition smoothly from one to the other. You'll notice the transition is applied to the original element, not the hover state. This is so that different states such as :active can also have different styles set and enjoy the transition. So remember, the transition declaration is added to the element it transitions *away* from. But how do transitions actually work?

The properties of a transition

A **transition** can be declared using up to four properties or a single shorthand declaration including all four:

- `transition-property`: the name of the CSS property to be transitioned (such as `background-color`, `text-shadow`, or `all` to transition every possible property).

- `transition-duration`: the length of time over which the transition should occur (defined in seconds, for example `.3s`, `2s`, or `1.5s`).

- `transition-timing-function`: how the transition changes speed during the duration (for example `ease`, `linear`, `ease-in`, `ease-out`, `ease-in-out`, or `cubic-bezier`).

- `transition-delay`: an optional value to determine a delay before the transition commences. Alternatively, a negative value can be used to commence a transition immediately but part way through its transition 'journey'.

Used separately, the various transition properties can be used to create a transition as follows:

```
#content a {
    ...(more styles)...
    transition-property: all;
    transition-duration: 1s;
    transition-timing-function: ease;
    transition-delay: 0s;
}
```

The transition shorthand property

As we've already seen however, we can roll these individual declarations into a single, shorthand version:

```
transition: all 1s ease 0s;
```

One important point to note when writing the shorthand version is that the first timing value given is always taken to be the `transition-duration`. The second timing value is taken to be the `transition-delay`.

As ever, it's important to use vendor prefixes. For example, a stack of vendor-prefixed versions of the prior shorthand declaration would be as follows:

```
-o-transition: all 1s ease 0s;
-ms-transition: all 1s ease 0s;
-moz-transition: all 1s ease 0s;
-webkit-transition: all 1s ease 0s;
transition: all 1s ease 0s;
```

We've placed the non-prefixed 'official' version last so it will overwrite the others when browsers have fully implemented the standard.

Limitations of transitions

There are some caveats to using transitions; some properties can't be transitioned, despite the specifications (even the latest editor's draft at http://dev.w3.org/csswg/css3-transitions/) saying it should be possible. For example, the background-gradient property. However, you can, in theory, transition all these properties (http://www.w3.org/TR/css3-transitions/#properties-from-css-).

Transition different properties over different periods of time

Where a rule has multiple properties declared you don't have to transition all of them in the same way. Consider this rule:

```
#content a {
    ...(more styles)...
    transition-property: border, color, text-shadow;
    transition-duration: 2s, 3s, 8s;
}
```

Here we have specified with the transition-property that we'd like to transition the border, color, and text-shadow. Then with the transition-duration declaration, we are stating that the border should transition over 2 seconds, the color over 3 seconds, and the text-shadow over 8 seconds. The comma-separated durations match the comma-separated order of the transition properties.

Understanding timing functions

Most of the transition properties are self-explanatory. We've covered the list of properties that can be (or should be!) transitioned. Durations and delays are set with seconds (for example 2s) so they're simple enough to understand but the one property that can cause some head scratching is the timing functions. Just what do ease, linear, ease-in, ease-out, ease-in-out, and cubic-bezier actually do? Each of them is actually a cubic-bezier-curve — essentially the same as an easing function. I realize that perhaps doesn't mean much to you either. So… this is one of those situations where words (and certainly this author's power to wield them well enough) struggle to offer a satisfactory explanation — much like if you have to give your other half a satisfactory explanation for why you've forgotten their birthday! Instead, I recommend you head over to http://cubic-bezier.com/.

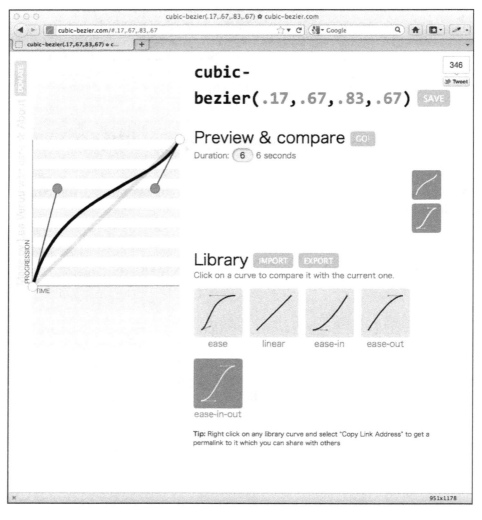

This site lets you compare timing functions and see the difference each one makes. However, even if you can write your own cubic-bezier curves blindfolded (while also counting backwards from a thousand in Mandarin), the likelihood is, for most practical situations, it makes little difference. Here's why…

Like any enhancement, it's necessary to employ transition effects subtly. For 'real world' implementations, transitions that occur over too great a period of time tend to make a site 'feel' slow. For example, navigation links that take 5 seconds to transition are going to frustrate, rather than 'Wow!' your users. Therefore, unless there is a compelling reason to do so, using the default transition (ease) over a short interval (a maximum of 1 second is my own preference) is often best.

Fun transitions for responsive web sites

Once you become a responsive web design junkie, you'll find yourself constantly resizing the browser window on websites you visit to see if it's responsive. Keep in mind this habit infuriates 'normal' people, so best only do it in private.

A great website I often visit that discusses CSS techniques is Chris Coyier's excellent `http://css-tricks.com`. After a re-design I happened to resize the browser window and smiled knowingly as the different on-screen elements whizzed about the screen. What magic had Chris employed to bring this effect about? Something similar to this:

```
* {
    transition: all 1s;
}
```

Here, we are using the CSS universal selector * to select everything and then setting a transition on `all` elements over 1 second (`1s`). As we have omitted to specify the timing function, `ease` will be used by default and there will be no delay as again, a default of none is assumed if an alternative value is not specifically added. The effect? Well, most things (links, hover states, and the like) behave as you would expect. However, because *everything* transitions, it also includes any rules within media queries, so as the browser window is resized, elements sort of flow from one state to the next. Is it essential? Absolutely not! Is it fun to watch and play around with? Certainly!

CSS3 2D transformations

Despite sounding similar, CSS **transformations** (both 2D and 3D variants) are entirely different to CSS transitions. Think of it like this: transitions smooth the change from one state to another, while transformations are defining what the element will become. My own (admittedly childish) way of remembering it is like this:

> *Imagine a Transformer robot like Optimus Prime. He's a robot that becomes something else (transforms) over a period of time (the transition) into a truck.*

In case that tangent muddied the waters further (or you don't have a clue who Optimus Prime is) let's just dig in. Let's add a 2D transition to the hover state of the navigation links on the **AND THE WINNER ISN'T** site:

```
nav ul li a:hover {
    transform: scale(1.7);
}
```

Now, in a modern browser, hovering over a link produces this effect:

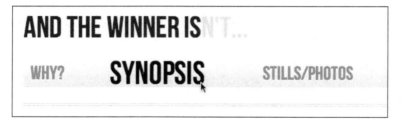

We've told the browser that when this element is hovered over, we want the element to scale to 1.7 times its original value.

Now, if you're attempting to add this rule to an element in Safari, be aware that it requires the main element to be displayed as a block. For example:

```
nav ul li a {
    height: 42px;
    text-decoration: none;
    text-transform: uppercase;
    color: black;
    text-shadow: 0 1px 0 hsla(0, 0%, 100%, 1.0);
    font: 1.875em/42px 'BebasNeueRegular';
    display: block;
}
```

Otherwise nothing happens, which is, you know, rubbish.

What can we transform?

There are two groups of CSS3 transforms available: 2D and 3D. 2D variants are far more widely implemented, browser wise, and certainly easier to write so let's look at those first. The CSS3 2D Transforms Module allows us to use the following transformations:

- `scale`: used to scale an element (larger or smaller)
- `translate`: move an element on the screen (up, down, left, and right)
- `rotate`: rotate the element by a specified amount (defined in degrees)
- `skew`: used to skew an element with its X and Y co-ordinates
- `matrix`: allows you to move and shape transformations with pixel precision

Let's try each of these and see what we can achieve.

scale

We've already looked at this transform above. However, besides the positive values we've already used, it's worth knowing that by using values below 1, we can shrink elements; the following will shrink the element to half its size:

```
transform: scale(0.5);
```

translate

```
transform: translate(40px, 0px);
```

`translate` tells the browser to move the element by an amount, defined in either pixels or percentages. The syntax is applied first from the left to the right (40px here) and then from the top to the bottom (0px here so it stays in line with the other navigation elements). Positive values given within parentheses move the element right or down; negative values move it left or up. So using this declaration on our navigation hover state results in this—our link shifting 40 pixels to the right when hovered over:

rotate

```
transform: rotate(90deg);
```

`rotate` allows you to rotate an element. In this example, we've amended the hover link to rotate 90 degrees. In the browser, here's what happens:

The value in parentheses should always be in degrees (for example, `90deg`). That doesn't stop you going crazy—you can make elements spin by specifying a value like the following:

```
transform: rotate(3600deg);
```

This will rotate the element 10 times in a complete circle. Practical uses for this particular value are few and far between but you know, if you ever find yourself designing websites for a windmill company it may come in handy!

skew

If you've spent any time working in Photoshop, you'll have a good idea what `skew` will do. It allows an element to be skewed on either or both of its axes.

```
transform: skew(10deg, 2deg);
```

Setting this on the hover link produces the following effect on hover:

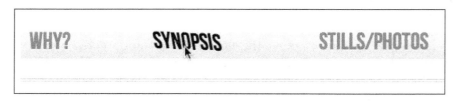

The first value is the skew applied to the X axis (in our example, `10deg`), while the second (`2deg`) is for the Y axis. Omitting the second value means any value will be applied to the X axis (horizontal). For example:

```
transform: skew(10deg);
```

This is perfectly valid but will only apply skew to the X axis. Values should always be given in degrees. While positive values always apply clockwise, using negative values will rotate the element counter-clockwise.

matrix

So, on the subject of over-rated films. What's that? You want to know about the CSS3 `matrix`, not the film? Oh, okay…

The `matrix` transform syntax looks scary:

```
transform: matrix(1.678, -0.256, 1.522, 2.333, -51.533, -1.989);
```

It essentially allows you to combine a number of other transforms (scale, rotate, skew, and so on) into a single declaration. The above declaration results in the following effect in the browser:

Now, I like a challenge like the best of them (unless, you know, it's sitting through Moulin Rouge) but I'm sure we can agree that syntax is a bit testing. It gets worse when you look at the specification and realize that it involves mathematics knowledge to fully understand: http://www.w3.org/TR/css3-2d-transforms/#cssmatrix-interface.

Matrix transformations for cheats and dunces

I'm not a mathematician by any stretch of the imagination so when faced with the need to create a matrix based transformation, I cheat. If your mathematical skills are also found wanting, I'd suggest heading over to http://www.useragentman.com/matrix/.

The **Matrix Construction Set** website allows you to drag and drop the element exactly where you want it and then includes good ol' copy and paste code (including vendor-prefixes) for your CSS file.

transform-origin property

Alongside the aforementioned transformations, you can use the `transform-origin` property to amend the point from which transforms are applied:

```
transform: rotate(45deg);
transform-origin: 20% 20%;
```

Setting this on our navigation links results in the following when hovered over:

The `transform-origin` property comes in useful as by default, transformations are applied to the center of an element. This provides a handy means of offsetting it and can produce some great results.

 Full information on the `transform-origin` property can be found here: http://www.w3.org/TR/css3-2d-transforms/#transform-origin-property

That covers the essentials of 2D transforms. They are far more widely implemented in the browser landscape than their 3D brethren and when used sensibly, provide a light-weight means of providing visual flourishes to reward users with modern browsers.

Read the full specification on **CSS3 2D Transforms Module Level 3** here: http://www.w3.org/TR/css3-2d-transforms/

Dabbling in CSS3 3D transformations

Although already supported by Webkit browsers (Safari and Chrome) and Firefox 10+, CSS3 3D transforms won't be supported in IE until version 10. However, despite a lack of support in 'desktop' browsers, thanks to their origin in Webkit, they are well supported in Android (v3 onwards) and iOS (all versions).

Suffice to say, from this point on, you'll be best off checking your results in a Webkit based browser such as Chrome or Safari (unless, of course, you're reading this at a time when your browser of choice *does* support 3D transformations).

Now, we're just going to dabble in 3D transformations here. They're a vast subject and the possibilities are virtually infinite. I imagine by the time they are supported widely, most of us will reach for them to create Carousel effects, rather than relying on JavaScript solutions from the likes of jQuery. However, until then, let's just open the lid and take a peek at what's possible.

Let's imagine we're making a simple quiz for the **AND THE WINNER ISN'T** website. It will be composed of images of movie posters and you have to guess whether they are considered 'Hot or Not' by the world's most respected film critic (yep, that's me). Hovering over the images (or tapping on a touch screen) will reveal the answer.

Here's the relevant section of markup; note that I've omitted the repetition of the markup for each image as they follow exactly the same format:

```
<section class="Qcontainer">
  <div class="film">
    <div class="face front">
      <img src="img/goonies.jpg" alt="The Goonies" />
    </div>
    <div class="face back"><h5>HOT!</h5></div>
  </div>
</section>
```

And now here's the CSS. Note, as Webkit is the browser with the greatest support for 3D transformations, the declarations here all use that specific vendor prefix. As ever, when implementing in the real world, vendor-prefixes are your friend.

```
.Qcontainer {
    height: 100%;
    width: 28%;
    position: relative;
    -webkit-perspective: 800;
    float: left;
    margin-right: 2%;
}
.film {
    width: 100%;
    height: 15em;
    -webkit-transform-style: preserve-3d;
    -webkit-transition: 1s;
```

```
}
.Qcontainer:hover .film {
    -webkit-transform: rotateY(180deg);
}
.face {
    position: absolute;
    -webkit-backface-visibility: hidden;
}
.back {
    width: 66%;
    height: 127%;
    -webkit-transform: rotateY(180deg);
    background: #3b3b3b;
    background: -webkit-linear-gradient(top,
                          rgba(0,0,0,0.65) 0%,
                          rgba(0,0,0,0) 100%);
    padding: 15%;
}
```

With that in place, hovering over the relevant image makes the poster flip and the simple **HOT** or **NOT** answer is revealed.

Breaking down the 3D effect

Let's go through the code to understand how this effect is achieved.

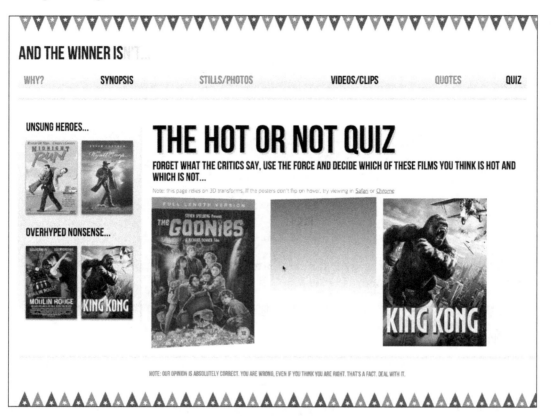

The first important point is to set the perspective on the parent element. This activates 3D space:

```
.Qcontainer {
    height: 100%;
    width: 28%;
    position: relative;
    -webkit-perspective: 200;
    float: left;
    margin-right: 2%;
}
```

The larger this perspective value, the greater the virtual depth of 3D space from your viewing point. Therefore, for a subtler 3D effect, increase the value. For a more dramatic effect, decrease it.

The next noteworthy point:

```
.film {
    width: 100%;
    height: 15em;
    -webkit-transform-style: preserve-3d;
    -webkit-transition: 1s;
}
```

The first perspective declaration added to the .Qcontainer class only applies to the first direct descendent (the div with a class of .film in this example). Therefore, to pass on the parent's perspective we use the preserve-3d value.

Now, we'll add a rule to flip the .film div when the .Qcontainer section is hovered over:

```
.Qcontainer:hover .film {
    -webkit-transform: rotateY(180deg);
}
```

The next rule deals with hiding the opposite side of the poster when it's flipped:

```
.face {
    position: absolute;
    -webkit-backface-visibility: hidden;
}
```

The absolute positioning on the .face is necessary to position it on top of the .back DIV:

```
.back {
    width: 66%;
    height: 127%;
    -webkit-transform: rotateY(180deg);
    background: #3b3b3b;
    background: -webkit-linear-gradient(top,
                            rgba(0,0,0,0.65) 0%,
                            rgba(0,0,0,0) 100%);
    padding: 15%;
}
```

Finally, we also add a simple rotateY on the .back DIV. Without this, the .back DIV effectively shows through the front.

And that's all there is to it. Now, hovering over any of the posters flips them in a rather dramatic fashion.

However, for any non-Webkit browsers the page functionality is decidedly lame:

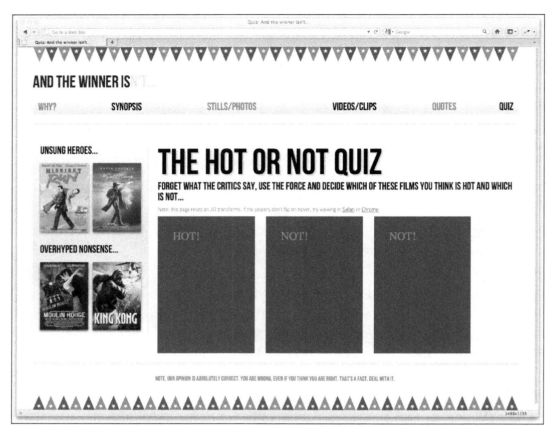

Well, we can provide an acceptable fallback for non-Webkit browsers with a little CSS of old:

```
.front {
    z-index: 5;
}
.Qcontainer:hover .front {
    z-index: 0;
}
```

First, we set a z-index of 5 on the .front DIV so that it sits above the .back DIV by default:

```
.front {
    z-index: 5;
}
```

Now, when the `.Qcontainer` section is hovered over, we'll set the `z-index` to `0` so it once more sits behind the `.back` DIV:

```
.Qcontainer:hover .front {
    z-index: 0;
}
```

Now we get a functional question and answer functionality in non-3D transform capable browsers, *sans* the fancy 3D effect.

3D transformations not ready for prime time

In my experience, at present, many of the 3D transforms don't play happily with percentage sizes (for example, amending the viewport width with the prior example makes things misbehave severely). So there's often quite a bit of tweaking to be done to make them play happily within a responsive layout. Furthermore, as support is currently so limited, 3D transformations seldom offer the most robust solution when you're building a cross-browser site. So for now, I still err towards jQuery or similar for this kind of functionality.

The possibilities of CSS 3D transforms are, however, extremely promising and when browser support is extended, they offer the opportunity to move many of the fancy effects we currently rely on JavaScript for, to be moved within our stylesheets.

 Read about the latest W3C developments on **CSS 3D Transforms** at `http://dev.w3.org/csswg/css3-3d-transforms/`

Animating with CSS3

If you've ever worked with Flash, you'll have an instant advantage when working with CSS3 animations. CSS3 employs animation keyframing conventions found in Flash and other timeline based applications.

Animations are also more widely implemented than 3D transforms. They are supported in Firefox 5+, Chrome, Safari 4+, Android (all versions), iOS (all versions), and due to be incorporated into Internet Explorer 10.

There are two components to a CSS3 animation; firstly a keyframes declaration and then using that keyframe declaration in an animation property. Let's take a look.

In the previous section we made a simple flip effect for films that I consider **HOT** or **NOT**. Well, the text on the reveal is pretty dull, so let's add a nice pulsing effect to the answer that's revealed after the poster flips.

Firstly the keyframe rule:

```
@keyframes warning {
  0% {
    text-shadow: 0px 0px 4px #000000;
  }
  50% {
    text-shadow: 0 0 20px #000000;
  }
  100% {
    text-shadow: 0px 0px 4px #000000;
  }
}
```

I'm using the non-prefixed version of the code here so if things aren't happening you'll probably need to add a full vendor-prefixed stack (@-webkit-keyframes for example).

Let's break this down:

```
@keyframes warning {
  0% {
    text-shadow: 0px 0px 4px #000000;
  }
  50% {
    text-shadow: 0 0 20px #000000;
  }
  100% {
    text-shadow: 0px 0px 4px #000000;
  }
}
```

First, we are specifying a @keyframes declaration. We are then giving this particular keyframes declaration a name—warning in this instance. You can name them however you like but as these keyframe declarations can be re-used on multiple elements, name them accordingly.

You can set as many percentage points as you like (for example, 10, 20, 30, 40, and so on) or if you'd rather, define the animation with from and to values. Be warned however that Webkit browsers don't always play happily with from and to values (preferring 0% and 100%):

```
@keyframes warning {
  from {
    text-shadow: 0px 0px 4px #000000;
  }
  50% {
    text-shadow: 0 0 40px #000000;
  }
  to {
    text-shadow: 0 0 4px #000000;
  }
}
```

In this instance I'm altering a text-shadow, starting and ending with the same distance of 4px but going to 40px blur at 50%.

Now we have declared the keyframe, we can reference it with the animation property:

```
.back h5 {
    font-size: 4em;
    color: #f2050b;
    text-align: center;
    animation: warning 1.5s infinite ease-in;
}
```

After specifying the animation property, we define the particular keyframe rule we want to use (`warning` in this case), we then specify the `animation-iteration-count` (we've used infinite here so the animation continues continuously) and finally the timing function (`ease-in`). A static image obviously fails to do this justice but hopefully you can imagine the text shadow pulsing back and forth. View this in the browser at `http://www.andthewinnerisnt.com`.

The shorthand property can accept all seven animation properties. In addition to those used in the above example, it's also possible to specify `animation-delay` (for example, if you wanted to delay when the animation starts), `animation-play-state` (can be set to `running` or `paused` to effectively play and pause an animation) and finally `animation-fill-mode`, which I confess, I've yet to find a need to use (the default is `none`). Of course you don't need to use the shorthand property; you can list them individually as follows:

```
animation-name: warning;
animation-duration: 1.5s;
animation-timing-function: ease-in-out;
animation-iteration-count: infinite;
animation-play-state: running;
animation-delay: 0s;
animation-fill-mode: none;
```

As mentioned previously, it's simple to reuse the animation on other elements. For example:

```
nav ul li a:hover {
    animation: warning 1.5s infinite ease-in;
}
```

This gives our navigation links the same pulsing effect. You can (hopefully) see the STILLS/PHOTOS link in the screenshot below in the midst of the animation. Try it out for yourself at `http://www.andthewinerisnt.com`.

This is just one very simple example of using CSS animations. As virtually anything can be key-framed, the possibilities are pretty endless. There are countless showcases of CSS3 animation techniques around the web. Pages like `http://webdesignerwall.com/trends/47-amazing-css3-animation-demos` should give you more than enough inspiration to be getting on with.

 Read about the latest developments on CSS3 Animations at `http://dev.w3.org/csswg/css3-animations/`.

Putting CSS3 transformations and animations together

Let's try one more thing to flex our CSS3 muscles. I'd like to try placing all the aside sidebar images at varying angles and then animating them. The aim is to have them 'shake' when the page is first visited. Here's the markup for the sidebar:

```
<aside>
  <div role="complementary">
    <div class="sideBlock unSung">
      <h1>Unsung heroes...</h1>
      <a href="#"><img src="img/midnightRun.jpg"
                  alt="Midnight Run" /></a>
      <a href="#"><img src="img/wyattEarp.jpg"
                  alt="Wyatt Earp" /></a>
    </div>
  </div>
  <div role="complementary">
    <div class="sideBlock overHyped">
      <h1>Overhyped nonsense...</h1>
      <a href="#"><img src="img/moulinRouge.jpg"
                  alt="Moulin Rouge" /></a>
      <a href="#"><img src="img/kingKong.jpg"
                  alt="King Kong" /></a>
    </div>
  </div>
</aside>
```

Now let's create the CSS3 to make this work. First, let's create a new keyframe declaration called `swing`:

```
@-webkit-keyframes swing {
  from {
    transform: rotate(3deg);
  }
  20% {
    transform: rotate(7deg);
  }
  60% {
    transform: rotate(10deg);
  }
  80% {
    transform: rotate(7deg);
  }
  to {
    transform: rotate(3deg);
  }
}
```

The animation will use the 2D rotate transform to move the item from 3 degrees to 10 and back again. And here's how the `animation` property is added:

```
#quiz .unSung a:nth-child(odd) img {
    transform: rotate(3deg);
    animation: swing 0.1s 5 ease-in;
}
#quiz .unSung a:nth-child(even) img {
    transform: rotate(-3deg);
    animation: swing 0.1s 5 0.3s ease-in;
}
#quiz .overHyped a:nth-child(odd) img {
    transform: rotate(3deg);
    animation: swing 0.1s 5 0.2s ease-in;
}
#quiz .overHyped a:nth-child(even) img {
    transform: rotate(-3deg);
    animation: swing 0.1s 5 0.5s ease-in;
}
```

Let's break this down. Firstly by relying on CSS specificity we can target these rules only at the **QUIZ** page (which has a `<body id="quiz">` tag).

Before adding the animation property, I want to set a default rotate transform so that they remain off-kilter when the animation completes. I don't want them all at the same angle—so let's use the `nth-child` selector we learned about in *Chapter 5, CSS3: Selectors, Typography, and Color Modes* to select the odd and even images and apply different rotation transforms to them:

```css
#quiz .unSung a:nth-child(odd) img {
    transform: rotate(3deg);
    animation: swing 0.1s 5 ease-in;
}
#quiz .unSung a:nth-child(even) img {
    transform: rotate(-3deg);
    animation: swing 0.1s 5 0.3s ease-in;
}
#quiz .overHyped a:nth-child(odd) img {
    transform: rotate(3deg);
    animation: swing 0.1s 5 0.2s ease-in;
}
#quiz .overHyped a:nth-child(even) img {
    transform: rotate(-3deg);
    animation: swing 0.1s 5 0.5s ease-in;
}
```

Then the `animation` property is added for each instance. You'll notice slight variations in each of the rules. The shorthand property also takes into account that the second time value given (`0.5s`) is assigned to the animation delay. By utilizing this value we can effectively fire off each different instance separately.

```css
#quiz .overHyped a:nth-child(even) img {
    transform: rotate(-3deg);
    animation: swing 0.1s 5 0.5s ease-in;
}
```

Again, when writing about animations, it's a little difficult to convey the effect. If you're not near an Internet connection, the best I can tell you is that the films rapidly shake from side to side and then settle off-kilter as shown in the following image:

Summary

It would be entirely possible to fill multiple books covering the possibilities of CSS transformations, transitions, and animations. However, hopefully, by dipping your toe in the water with this chapter you'll be able to pick up the basics and run with them. Ultimately, by embracing the new features and techniques of CSS3 the aim is to make a responsive design even leaner and richer than ever by using CSS3, rather than JavaScript for some of the fancier aesthetic enhancements. In this chapter we've learned what CSS3 transitions are and how to write them, got a handle on timing functions like 'ease' and 'linear', and then used them to create simple but fun effects with our responsive design. We then learned all about 2D transformations like scale and skew and then how to use them in tandem with transitions. We also looked briefly at 3D transformations before learning all about the power and relative simplicity of CSS animations. You'd better believe our CSS3 muscles are growing!

However, if there's one area of site design that I always avoid where possible (as desperately as I avoid *Munich* or *King Kong* if they're showing), it's making forms. I don't know why, I've just always found making them a tedious and frustrating task. Imagine my joy when I learned that HTML5 and CSS3 can make the whole form building, styling, and even validating (yes, validating!) process easier than ever before. I was quite joyous. As joyous as you can be about building web forms that is. In the next chapter I'd like to share this knowledge with you.

8
Conquer Forms with HTML5 and CSS3

Historically, forms have been a pain to style consistently cross-browser. They also require JavaScript to validate the inputs and lack specific input types to deal with everyday information like telephone numbers, e-mail addresses, and URLs.

The good news is that HTML5 largely solves these common problems. Let's get familiar with the new HTML5 form features and see how they alleviate our traditional form-building burden.

Using HTML5 to code our forms brings an additional benefit when used for responsive designs; it once more allows us to trim our code base to provide the leanest possible pages for our users. For the browsers that don't support these new features, we have tools to patch them up and bring them in line.

In this chapter, we will learn how to use HTML5 to:

- Easily insert placeholder text into relevant form fields
- Disable auto-completion of form fields where necessary
- Set certain fields to be required before submission
- Specify different input types such as e-mail, telephone number, and URL
- Create number range sliders for easy value selection
- Insert date and color pickers
- Learn how we can use a regular expression to define an allowed form value
- Add a polyfill to provide support for less capable browsers
- Use CSS3 to easily and flexibly style an HTML5 form

HTML5 forms

Here's the scenario: for our example *And the winner isn't...* responsive website. I've decided that I'd like people to be able to vent their own frustration at the turkeys that have been picking up the award gongs. We'll be adding a form that let's people tell us about the film they feel shouldn't have won, and the film they feel should have taken its place.

The following screenshot shows how our basic form looks, with just a little basic styling in Chrome (v16):

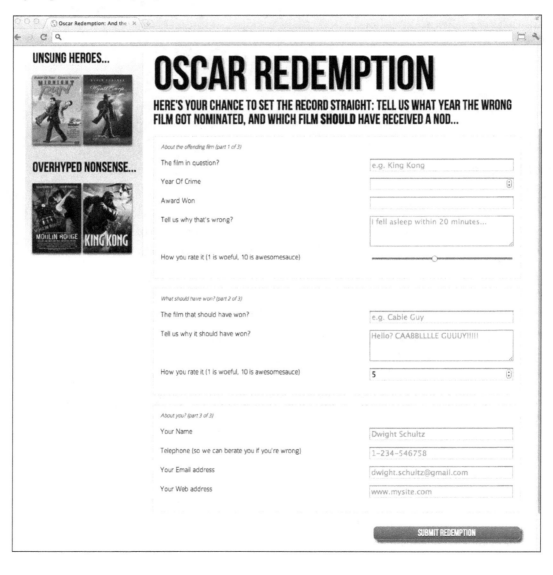

Besides standard form input fields and text areas, we have a number spinner, a range slider, and placeholder text for many of the fields. If we 'focus' (select) on that particular field the placeholder text is removed and if we lose focus without entering anything (by clicking outside of the input box again) the placeholder text re-appears. Furthermore, looking at this page in Google's Chrome browser, if we go ahead and submit the form without entering anything, the following happens:

So besides a couple of visual flourishes (the slider and spinner) we have some client-side validation in place. As we've already noted, typically, to get a form working like this would require JavaScript of one sort or another.

However, the great news is that all these user interface elements (including the aforementioned slider, placeholder text, and spinner) and the form validation are all being handled natively with HTML5 and no JavaScript is being employed. Let's work through how the new form capabilities of HTML5 make this possible.

Understanding the component parts of HTML5 forms

There's a lot going on in our HTML5 powered form, so let's break it down. The form has been given an ID to aid styling and then an HTML5 hgroup for the title and introductory text:

```
<form id="redemption" method="post">
  <hgroup>
    <h1>Oscar Redemption</h1>
    <h2>Here's your chance to set the record straight: tell us what
      year the wrong film got nominated, and which film <b>should</b>
      have received a nod...</h2>
  </hgroup>
```

The three sections of the form are then wrapped in a fieldset with a legend:

```
<fieldset>
<legend>About the offending film (part 1 of 3)</legend>
<div>
  <label for="film">The film in question?</label>
  <input id="film" name="film" type="text" placeholder="e.g. King
    Kong" required aria-required="true" >
</div>
```

You can see from the previous code snippet that each input element of the form is also wrapped in a div with a label associated with each input. So far, so normal. However, within this first input we've just stumbled upon our first HTML5 form features. After common attributes of id, name, and type we have placeholder.

placeholder

The placeholder attribute looks similar to the following:

```
placeholder="e.g. King Kong"
```

Placeholder text within form fields is such a common requirement that the folks creating HTML5 decided it should be built into the markup and supported by browsers. Simply include the placeholder attribute within your input and the value will be displayed by default until the field gains focus. When it loses focus, if a value has not been entered, it will re-display the placeholder text.

After the placeholder attribute, in the previous code snippet, the next HTML5 form feature is the `required` attribute.

required

The required attribute looks similar to the following:

```
required aria-required="true"
```

In supporting HTML5 capable browsers, by adding the Boolean (meaning you simply include the attribute or not) attribute `required` within the input element, it indicates that a value is required. If the form is submitted without the field containing the requisite information, a warning message should be displayed. The message displayed is specific (both in content and styling) to both the browser and the input type used. In addition to the HTML5 `required` value, in our example we have also added the WAI-ARIA equivalent; `aria-required="true"`. Unless there is a good reason not to, include this WAI-ARIA version of the required attribute to assist those using screen readers (if you remember, we looked at WAI-ARIA back in *Chapter 4, HTML5 for Responsive Designs*).

We've already seen what the `required` field browser message looks like in Chrome. The following screenshot shows the same message in Firefox (9):

The `required` value can be used alongside many input types to ensure a value is entered. Notable exceptions are the `range`, `color`, `button`, and `hidden` input types as they almost always have a default value.

Another HTML5 form attribute that can be added to input fields is `autofocus`.

autofocus

The HTML5 `autofocus` attribute allows a form to be loaded with a field already focused (selected) ready for user input. The following code is an example of an input field wrapped in a `div` with the autofocus attribute added at the end:

```
<div>
  <label for="search">Search the site...</label>
  <input id="search" name="search" type="search" placeholder="Wyatt
    Earp" autofocus>
</div>
```

Be careful when using this attribute. Cross browser confusion can reign if multiple fields have the autofocus attribute added. For example, if multiple fields have `autofocus` added, in Chrome (v16) the last field with the `autofocus` attributed is focused on page load. However, Firefox (v9) does the opposite with the first `autofocus` field selected.

It's also worth considering that some users use the space bar to quickly skip down the content of a web page once it's loaded. On a page where a form has an autofocused input field, it prevents this capability; instead it adds a space into the focused input field. It's easy to see how that could be a source of frustration for users.

autocomplete

By default, most browsers aid user input by autocompleting the value of form fields where possible. Whilst the user can turn this preference on and off within the browser, we can now also indicate to the browser when we don't want a form or field to allow auto-completion. This is useful not just for sensitive data (for example bank account numbers) but also if you want to ensure users pay attention and enter something *by hand*. For example, for many forms I complete, if a telephone number is required, I enter a 'spoof' telephone number. I know I'm not the only one that does that (doesn't everyone?) but I can ensure that users don't enter an autocompleted spoof number by setting the autocomplete attribute to off on the relevant input field. The following is a code example of a field with the autocomplete attribute set to `off`:

```
<div>
  <label for="tel">Telephone (so we can berate you if you're
    wrong)</label>
  <input id="tel" name="tel" type="tel" placeholder="1-234-546758"
    autocomplete="off" required aria-required="true" >
</div>
```

We can also set entire forms (but not fieldsets) to not autocomplete by using the attribute on the form itself. The following is a code example:

```
<form id="redemption" method="post" autocomplete="off">
```

list (and the associated datalist element)

This list attribute and the associated datalist element allow a number of selections to be presented to a user once they start entering a value in the field. The following is a code example of the list attribute in use with an associated datalist wrapped in a div:

```
<div>
  <label for="awardWon">Award Won</label>
  <input id="awardWon" name="awardWon" type="text" list="awards">
  <datalist id="awards">
    <select>
      <option value="Best Picture"></option>
      <option value="Best Director"></option>
      <option value="Best Adapted Screenplay"></option>
      <option value="Best Original Screenplay"></option>
    </select>
  </datalist>
</div>
```

The value given in the list attribute (awards) refers to the id of the datalist. Doing this associates the datalist with the input field. Although wrapping the options with a <select> element isn't strictly necessary, it helps when applying polyfills for older browsers.

Whilst the input field seems to be just a normal text input field, when typing in the field, a selection box appears below it (in supporting browsers) with matching results from the datalist. In the following screenshot, we can see the list in action (Firefox v9). In this instance, as **B** is present in all options within the datalist, all values are shown to select from:

However, when typing **D** instead, only the matching suggestions appear as shown in the following screenshot:

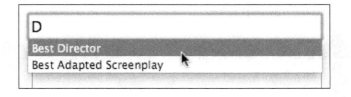

This doesn't prevent a user entering anything else they want in the input box but it provides another great way of adding common functionality and user enhancement through markup alone.

HTML5 input types

HTML5 adds a number of extra input types, which amongst other things, enable us to limit the data that users input without the need for extraneous JavaScript code. The most comforting thing about these new input types is that by default, where browsers don't support the feature, they degrade to a standard text input box. Furthermore, there are great polyfills available to bring older browsers up to speed. We will look at these shortly. In the meantime, let's look at these new HTML5 input types and the benefits they provide.

email

`type="email"` – supporting browsers will expect a user input that matches the syntax of an e-mail address. In the following code example `type="email"` is used alongside `'required'` and `'placeholder'`:

```
<div>
  <label for="email">Your Email address</label>
  <input id="email" name="email" type="email" placeholder=
    "dwight.schultz@gmail.com" required aria-required="true">
</div>
```

When used in conjunction with `required` submitting a non-conforming input will generate a warning message:

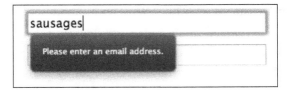

Furthermore, many touch screen devices (for example Android, iPhone and so on) change the input display based upon this input type. The following screenshot shows how an input `type="email"` screen looks on the iPad. Notice the '@' symbol for easy email address completion:

number

`type="number"` – supporting browsers expect a number to be entered in a number type input field. They also supply *spinner* controls by default, allowing users to easily click up or down to alter the value. The following is a code example:

```
<div>
  <label for="yearOfCrime">Year Of Crime</label>
  <input id="yearOfCrime" name="yearOfCrime" type="number" min="1929"
    max="2015" required aria-required="true" >
</div>
```

And the following screenshot shows how it looks in a supporting browser (Chrome v16):

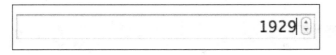

Implementation of what happens if you don't enter a number varies. For example, Chrome (v16) clears the field as soon as it loses focus without providing any feedback whilst Firefox (v9) allows anything to be entered (defaulting to the standard text input type). You'll notice in the previous code example, we have also set a minimum and maximum allowed range similar to the following code:

```
type="number" min="1929" max="2015"
```

Numbers outside of this range (should) get special treatment. Browser implementation is varied. For example, Chrome (v16) displays a warning whilst Firefox (v9) does nothing.

url

`type="url"` – as you might expect, the URL input type is for URL values. Similar to the `tel` and `email` input types, it behaves almost identically to a standard text input. However, some browsers add specific information to the warning message provided when submitted with incorrect values. The following is a code example including the `placeholder` attribute:

```
<div>
  <label for="web">Your Web address</label>
  <input id="web" name="web" type="url" placeholder="www.mysite.com">
</div>
```

The following screenshot shows what happens when an incorrectly entered URL field is submitted in Chrome (v16):

Like `type="email"`, touch screen devices often amend the input display based upon this input type. The following screenshot shows how an input `type="url"` screen looks on the iPad:

Notice the **Go**, forward slash (*/*), and **.com** keys? Because we've used a URL input type they are presented by the device for easy URL completion (unless you're not going to a .com site in which case, you know, thanks for nothing Apple).

tel

`type="tel"` is another contact information specific input type. `tel` is used to signify to the browser that the form expects a telephone number entered within that field. The following code is an example:

```
<div>
  <label for="tel">Telephone (so we can berate you if you're
    wrong)</label>
  <input id="tel" name="tel" type="tel" placeholder="1-234-546758"
    autocomplete="off" required aria-required="true" >
</div>
```

Although, a number format is expected, on many browsers, even modern ones such as Chrome v16 and Firefox v9, it merely behaves like a text input field. They are currently failing to provide a suitable warning message on form submission when incorrect values are entered.

However, better news is that like the email and url input types, touch screen devices often thoughtfully accommodate this kind of input with an amended input display for easy completion; here's the tel input when accessed with an iPad (running iOS 5):

Notice the lack of alphabet characters in the keyboard area? This makes it much faster for users to enter a value in the correct format.

search

`type="search"` – although the `search` input type works in the same manner as a standard text input, some browsers render the code with some subtle differences. The following code is an example:

```
<div>
  <label for="search">Search the site...</label>
  <input id="search" name="search" type="search" placeholder=
    "Wyatt Earp">
</div>
```

The following screenshot shows how the previous code looks in Firefox (v9); notice the default styling of the input box is rectangular:

Search the site... | Wyatt Earp

However, Chrome (v16) renders that same code differently by default with rounded edges and a quick clear button on the right:

pattern

`pattern=""` — *Be afraid, be very afraid* (remember what film that's the tagline from?) In my opinion, this tagline could just as easily be applied to **regular expressions**. If you don't know what regular expressions are, I dare say ignorance is bliss. If you do, and worse still, you understand them, the following section is for you.

Learn about regular expressions

If you've watched 'The Exorcist' alone, in a graveyard, at midnight, on Halloween you're possibly ready to learn about regular expressions: http://en.wikipedia.org/wiki/Regular_expressions.

The `pattern` attribute allows you to specify, via a regular expression, the syntax of data that should be allowed in a given input field. The following code is an example:

```
<div>
  <label for="name">Your Name (first and last)</label>
  <input id="name" name="name" pattern="([a-zA-Z]{3,30}\s*)+[a-zA-
    Z]{3,30}" placeholder="Dwight Schultz" required aria-
    required="true" >
</div>
```

Such is my commitment to this book, I searched the Internet for approximately 458 seconds to find a regular expression that would match a first and last name syntax. By entering the regular expression value within the `pattern` attribute, it makes supporting browsers expect a matching input syntax. Then, when used in conjunction with the `required` attribute, incorrect entries get the following treatment in supporting browsers. In this instance I tried submitting the form without providing a last name:

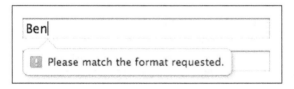

color

`type="color"` – the `color` input type produces a color picker in supporting browsers, allowing users to select a color value in a Hexadecimal value. The following code is an example:

```
<div>
  <label for="color">Your favorite color</label>
  <input id="color" name="color" type="color">
</div>
```

Sadly, at present, browser support is scant. Only Opera (v11) seems to provide the color picker. When the required color isn't initially shown, clicking the **Other...** button at the bottom launches the OS's default color picker:

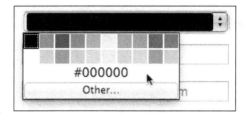

Date and time inputs

The thinking behind the new `date` and `time` input types is to provide a consistent user experience for choosing dates and times. If you've ever bought tickets to an event online, chances are that you have used a date picker of one sort or another. This functionality is almost always provided via JavaScript (typically jQuery) but the hope is to make this common necessity possible merely with HTML5 markup.

date

The following code is an example:

```
<input id="date" type="date" name="date" />
```

Similar to the `color` input type, native browser support is thin on the ground at present, defaulting on most browsers to a standard text input box. Good ol' Opera has already implemented the functionality though and the following screenshot shows how that example code renders in Opera (v11):

There are a variety of different `date` and `type` input types available. What follows is a brief overview of the others.

month

The following code is an example:

```
<input id="month" type="month" name="month">
```

The interface allows the user to select a single month and provides the input as a year and month for example **2012-06**.

The following screenshot shows how it looks in the browser:

week

The following code is an example:

```
<input id="week" type="week" name="week">
```

When the `week` input type is used, the picker allows the user to select a single week within a year and provides the input in the **2012-W47** format.

The following screenshot shows how it looks in the browser:

time

The following code is an example:

```
<input id="time" type="time" name="time">
```

The `time` input type allows a value in the 24 hour format, for example **23:50**.

It displays in supporting browsers with spinner controls but only allows relevant time values:

datetime and datetime-local

The following code is an example:

```
<input id="datetime" type="datetime" name="datetime">
```

It looks similar to the following screenshot in Opera (v11):

And looks even better on iOS devices as shown in the following screenshot:

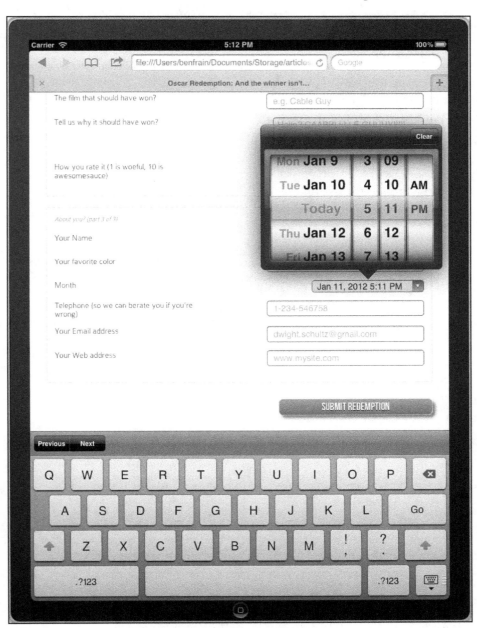

This input type creates date and time values (separated by a T) and then the time zone (**Z** for UTC or a + or – for offset values). 25th October 2009 in UTC is shown as follows:

2009-10-25T05:05:00Z

As UTC is, for most practical purposes, equivalent to GMT, it's easy to understand offsets. For example, Pacific Standard Time (Los Angeles) is 8 hours behind GMT (UTC -8 hours). That would be reflected in the input value as shown:

2009-10-25T05:05:00-8:00

The datetime-local version works in exactly the same manner as datetime but omits the time zone information.

> **Changing the step increments**
>
> You can alter the step increments (granularity) for the spinner controls of various input types with the use of the step attribute. For example, to step 4 at a time, enter the value of 4 hours as 14400 seconds (60 (seconds), multiplied by 60 (minutes), multiplied by 4 (hours)). Following is the datetime example amended to use 4-hour steps in the time selector:
>
> <input id="datetime" type="datetime" name="datetime" step="14400">

range

The range input type creates a slider interface element. The following code is an example:

```
<input id="howYouRateIt" name="howYouRateIt" type="range" min="1"
   max="10" value="5" >
```

And the following screenshot shows how it looks in Safari (v5.1):

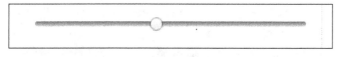

The default range is from 0 to 100. However, by specifying a min and max value in our example we have limited it to between 1 and 10.

One big problem I've encountered with the range input type is that the current value is never displayed to the user. Although the range slider is only intended for vague number selections, I've often wanted to display the value as it changes. Currently, there is no way to do this using HTML5. However, if you absolutely must display the current value of the slider, it can be achieved easily with some simple JavaScript. Amend the previous example to the following code:

```
<input id="howYouRateIt" name="howYouRateIt" type="range" min="1"
  max="10"value="5" onchange="showValue(this.value)"><span
  id="range">5</span>
```

We've added two things, an `onchange` attribute and also a `span` element with the id of `range`. Now, we'll add the following tiny piece of JavaScript somewhere in the page:

```
<script>
  function showValue(newValue)
  {
    document.getElementById("range").innerHTML=newValue;
  }
</script>
```

All this does is gets the current value of the range slider and display it in the element with an `id` of range (our span tag). With a tiny bit of CSS styling to make the value bigger and red, the following screenshot shows the effect–with the value updating as the slider is moved:

How you rate it (1 is woeful, 10 is awesomesauce)

8

There are a few other form related features that are new in HTML5 but as they relate more to building applications and backend development they've not been featured here. To read the *W3C Editor's draft of the HTML5 form section* visit: `http://dev.w3.org/html5/spec-author-view/forms.html#forms`.

How to polyfill non-supporting browsers

All this HTML5 form malarkey is all well and good. There seems however, to be two things that put a serious dent in our ability to use them: disparity between how supporting browsers implement the features and how to deal with browsers that don't support the features at all. Thankfully, as ever, the web community has found a way.

Back in *Chapter 4, HTML5 for Responsive Designs* I mentioned Modernizr (http:// www.modernizr.com), a fantastic JavaScript library that helps insert **polyfills** for browsers lacking the requisite HTML5/CSS3 features. *"Webshims Lib"*, written by *Alexander Farkas* (http://afarkas.github.com/webshim/demos/) is built on top of this and the ubiquitous jQuery library to only load the form polyfills (it can handle poly-filling of other HTML5 features too) needed to make non-supporting browsers handle our HTML5 forms. What's particularly great is the fact that as it utilizes Modernizr's loading capabilities, the relevant polyfills are only added if needed. It adds very little flab to a web page if being viewed by a browser that supports these HTML5 features natively. Older browsers, although they need to load more code (as they are less capable by default), get a similar user experience, albeit with the relevant functionality created with the help of JavaScript.

But it isn't just older browsers that benefit. As we've seen, many modern browsers haven't implemented the HTML5 form features fully. Employing Webshims Lib to the page also fills any gaps in their capability. For example, Safari (5.1) doesn't offer any warning when a HTML5 form is submitted with any required fields empty. Whilst the form isn't actually submitted, no feedback is given to the user as to what the problem is: hardly ideal. With Webshims Lib added to the page, the following happens in the aforementioned scenario:

So when Firefox (v9) isn't able to provide a spinner for a type="number" attribute, Webshims Lib provides a suitable jQuery powered fallback. In short, it's a great tool, so let's get this beautiful little package installed and hooked up and then we can carry on writing forms with HTML5, safe in the knowledge all users will see what they need to use our form (except those two people using IE6 with JavaScript turned off—you know who you are—now pack it in!).

First download Webshims Lib (http://github.com/aFarkas/webshim/downloads) and extract the package. Now copy the js-webshim folder to a relevant section of your web page. For simplicity, for this example I've copied it into the website root.

Now add the following code into the <head> section of your page:

```
<script src="js/jquery-1.7.1.js"></script>
<script src="js-webshim/minified/extras/modernizr-
  custom.js"></script>
<script src="js-webshim/minified/polyfiller.js"></script>
<script>
  //load all defined
  $.webshims.polyfill();
</script>
```

Let's go through this a section at a time. First I've linked to a local copy of the jQuery library (get the latest version at www.jquery.com):

```
<script src="js/jquery-1.7.1.js"></script>
```

Next, I'm adding the versions of Modernizr and the polyfiller JavaScript files that are within Webshims Lib:

```
<script src="js-webshim/minified/extras/modernizr-custom.js"></script>
<script src="js-webshim/minified/polyfiller.js"></script>
```

Finally, I'm telling the script to load all needed polyfills:

```
<script>
  //load all defined
  $.webshims.polyfill();
</script>
```

And that's all there is to it. Now, missing functionality is automatically added by the relevant polyfill. Excellent!

Styling HTML5 forms with CSS3

Our form is now fully functional across all browsers and whilst we've got some very basic styling, you and I both know, with CSS3 we can do so much better. Let's apply some of the techniques we've already learned and used to spice up our form a little. So far, the following are all the form specific styles we have:

```
#redemption {
  width: 100%;
  font-family: 'ColaborateThinRegular';
  font-weight: 400;
```

```
}
#redemption hgroup {
  margin-bottom: 20px;
}
#redemption div {
  width: 100%;
  margin-bottom: 15px;
  float: left;
}
#redemption span#range {
  float: left;
  font-size: 3em;
  width: 100%;
  color: red;
  clear: both;
  text-align: center;
}
#howYouRateThis,#yearOfCrime {
  text-align: right;
}
#redemption legend {
  font-style: italic;
  color: #434242;
  font-size: 0.8em;
  margin-bottom: 20px;
  float: left;
  width: 100%;
}
#redemption fieldset {
  border: 1px dotted #cccccc;
  padding: 2%;
  margin-bottom: 20px;
}
#redemption label {
  width: 40%;
  float: left;
}
#redemption input {
  height: 20px;
  font-size: 1em;
  width: 40%;
  float: right;
}
#redemption textarea {
```

```
    height: 60px;
    font-size: 1em;
    width: 40%;
    float: right;
}
#redemption input#submit {
    text-decoration: none;
    height: 34px;
    font: 1.25em /* 36px ÷ 16 */ 'BebasNeueRegular';
    background-color: #b01c20;
    border-radius: 8px;
    color: white;
    float: right;
    margin-bottom: 10px;
    background: linear-gradient(top, rgb(241,92,96) 0%, rgb(176,28,32)
        100%);
    margin-top: 10px;
    box-shadow: 5px 5px 5px hsla(0, 0%, 26.6667%, 0.8);
    text-shadow: 0px 1px black;
    border: 1px solid #bfbfbf;
}
.polyfill-important .input-range,.polyfill-important .step-controls {
    float: right;
}
.polyfill-important .step-controls {
    margin-right: -20px!important;
}
```

The only point worthy of note here is that the final two styles are only relevant when some of the polyfills are loaded.

So, first off, I want to make each fieldset stand out a little more with a subtle gradient background. The following is the amended CSS for the fieldset:

```
#redemption fieldset {
    border: 1px dotted #cccccc;
    padding: 2%;
    margin-bottom: 20px;
    background: #ffffff;
    background: linear-gradient(top, #ffffff 77%,#f2f2f2 100%);
    border-radius: 4px;
    box-shadow: 2px 2px 5px hsla(0, 0%, 16.6667%, 0.3);
}
```

Aside from the `border-radius`, and `background` gradient, the only other thing we have done is add a subtle `box-shadow` declaration.

As in many of the previous examples, I've omitted vendor-prefixed versions of the CSS3 declarations (background gradient, border-radius, and box-shadow in this case).

The following screenshot is the output shown in Chrome:

Mixing color values

Throughout the examples you can see that I've mixed and matched how colors have been defined. In some instances I'm using values like `red` whilst I've also used HEX, RGB and HSL values too. In supporting browsers there is no penalty for doing so. In a production site however, you may choose to stick to one or two formats for consistency.

So far, so good. But those text input fields are still looking a little drab. Let's add a sprinkling of CSS3 there too using the following code:

```
input, textarea, select {
  border: 1px solid #bfbfbf;
  padding: 0.2em;
  font-size: 1.1em;
  line-height: 1.2em;
  background: #ffffff;
  background: linear-gradient(top, #ffffff 0%,#ededed 8%,#ffffff
    100%);
  border-radius: 4px;
  box-shadow: 2px 2px 5px hsla(0, 0%, 16.6667%, 0.1);
}
```

Again, we've got a `background gradient` there, a slight `border-radius`, and a subtle `box-shadow`. The following screenshot shows how it looks in Chrome:

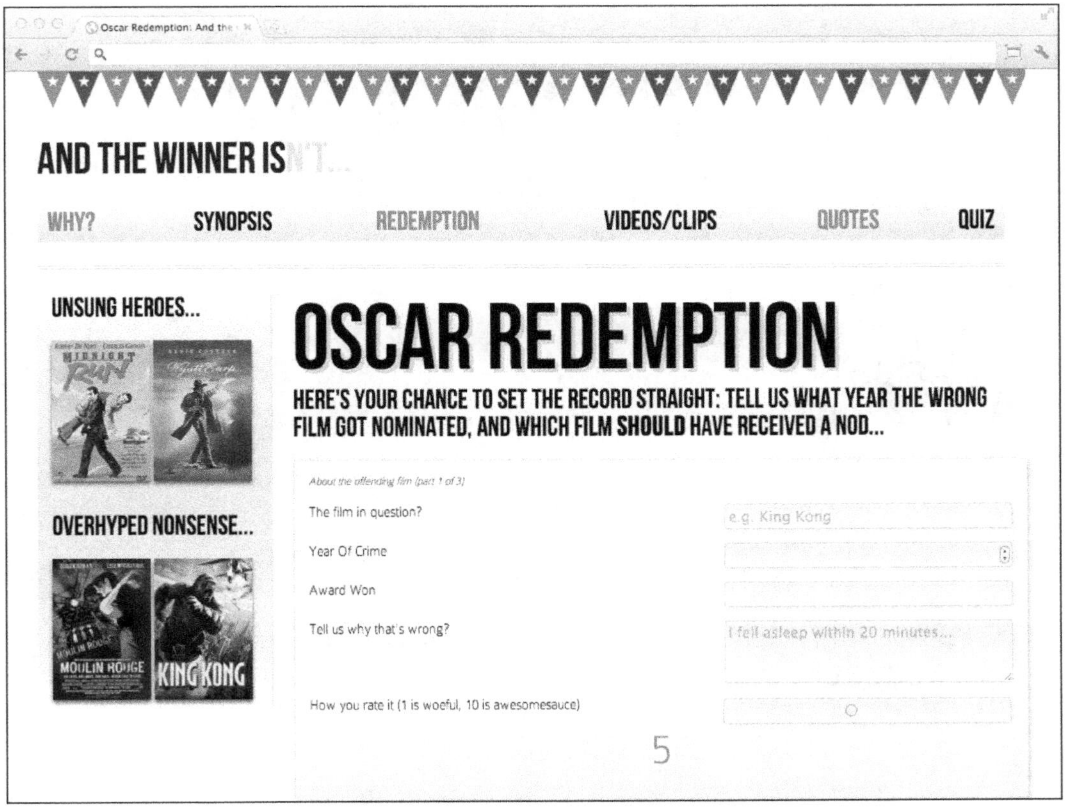

I'm happy with that…Oh, hold on. Take a look at the slider at the bottom. That's not what I want. I don't want those rules to affect the range slider so I'll amend my selector and use one of the new CSS3 selectors to sort things out:

```
input:not([type="range"]), textarea, select{
  /* the styles */
}
```

I've used the `:not` pseudo selector to specify that I don't want the rule to apply to inputs with the attribute `type="range"`. Let's take another look in Chrome:

Excellent! That's what I was gunning for and CSS3 has made it easy to not only add the relevant styles, but also to prevent adding them to elements on which they're not wanted.

Form-specific CSS3 pseudo class selectors

Alongside all the fun CSS3 tools we already know about, there are also a few form-specific pseudo selectors:

- `input:required`: for required fields
- `input:focus:invalid`: for focused fields that have an invalid value
- `input:focus:valid`: for focused fields that have a valid value

So, let's use these to make three additional style rules as shown in the following code examples:

```
input:required {
  border: 1px solid rgba(253, 8, 8, 0.29);
}
input:focus:invalid {
  background: url('../img/cross.png') no-repeat right;
  padding-right: 3px;
}
input:focus:valid {
  background: url('../img/tick.png') no-repeat right;
  padding-right: 3px;
}
```

The first is a subtle border for required fields. The second adds a cross for when an incorrect value has been included as the user types and the final rule adds a green tick when a correct value has been entered.

The following screenshot shows how that works in the browser (Firefox v9) on page load:

Now, if we focus (click into) on one of the required input fields, a **red cross** appears (as we haven't yet entered a valid value):

If we go ahead and enter a valid value, the **red cross** image swaps out for our **green tick**:

Using these new CSS3 pseudo class selectors makes for a nice, easy to implement, layer of enhancement that adds to the overall user experience when filling in the forms.

Summary

In this chapter, we have learned how to use a host of new HTML5 form attributes. They enable us to make forms more usable than ever before and the data they capture more relevant. Furthermore, we can future proof this new markup by using JavaScript feature detection and conditional loading of JavaScript polyfill scripts so that all users experience similar form features, regardless of their browsers capability.

We're nearing the end of our Responsive HTML5 and CSS3 journey. We've covered a lot of theory alongside our practical 'And the winner isn't' example website. However, implementing responsive designs in the real world often presents further challenges. How to handle a mass of navigation links on a small screen? How to only load additional files for the browsers that need them? In the final chapter we will be looking at some of these common issues (and their solutions) when implementing responsive designs built with HTML5 and CSS3. We'll also revisit how best to deal with some specific shortcomings of common older browsers.

9
Solving Cross-browser Responsive Challenges

In this final chapter, we will learn:

- The fundamental difference between progressive enhancement and graceful degradation
- How to make older versions of Internet Explorer responsive
- How to use Modernizr to conditionally load CSS files
- How to use Modernizr to conditionally load JavaScript polyfills
- How to change long lists of navigation to select menus on small viewports
- How to provide images for high resolution (retina) displays

Before we get to the meat of this final chapter, let's recap where we are and what we know.

Mobile usage is exploding. Consequently users view websites with a variety of viewports (different sizes and orientations) and with varying bandwidths. For the foreseeable future, we need to design and build our websites starting with the essential content and layering on features and enhancements progressively. Furthermore, due to the bandwidth considerations, the code base should be as lean and flexible as possible.

Design-wise, we've embraced all three legs of the Ethan Marcotte responsive design methodology. CSS3's media queries (covered in *Chapter 2, Media Queries: Supporting Differing Viewports*) are used to create design breakpoints where the layout can adapt dramatically to the viewport. Then flexible images and media alongside a fluid grid (covered in *Chapter 3, Embracing Fluid Layouts*) to provide a smooth flex between these media query breakpoints. The result is a design that not only works for today's popular viewports but for the future's too.

To keep our code base lean, in *Chapter 4, HTML5 for Responsive Designs*, we switched our markup to HTML5. It provides economies, more semantic code, and makes features such as offline viewing possible. Going further, we added some WAI-ARIA accessibility to our code, providing additional aids for screen readers and assistive technologies.

In *Chapter 5, CSS3: Selectors, Typography, and Color Modes* and *Chapter 6, Stunning Aesthetics with CSS3*, we looked at the incredible power and flexibility of CSS3, learning about new RGBA and HSLA color modes and how common design flourishes such as box-shadows, text-shadows, background gradients, and so on can be achieved without images, using CSS3 alone. In addition, the powerful selectors of CSS3 have allowed us to select anything we need from the DOM, a level of selection power that previously required JavaScript. Yet CSS3 hasn't just given us the ability to adapt the design and drastically lower the amount of bandwidth required to view our site. It has also added functionality we could never enjoy before without employing Flash of JavaScript: custom typography (*Chapter 5, CSS3: Selectors, Typography, and Color Modes*) and beautiful smooth transitions (*Chapter 7, CSS3 Transitions, Transformations, and Animations*) between different visual states. Keeping one eye on the future, we also glimpsed at sophisticated features such as CSS3 3D transformations.

Finally, in the last chapter, we tackled the humdrum task of form building, relishing the opportunity to handle the heavy work of form validation and form UI element creation using HTML5 markup. Importantly, we also added a JavaScript fall back to conditionally enhance the experience for older browsers such as Internet Explorer versions 6, 7, and 8.

Throughout this book we've built up a fairly simple responsive website in HTML and CSS3 called *And The Winner Isn't...*. You can visit this site in your browser at `http://www.andthewinerisnt.com`.

The following screenshot shows how the front page currently looks on an iPhone:

The following screenshot shows how the front page looks on an iPad:

The following screenshot shows how it looks in the Android browser (emulator):

The following screenshot shows how it looks in a modern desktop browser (Google Chrome v16):

Finally, the following screenshot shows how it looks presently in Internet Explorer 8:

Oh Momma! Pass the service revolver...

Looking at the site in Internet Explorer 8, which doesn't understand HTML5 elements, such as `<aside>`, `<header>`, `<nav>`, and `<footer>`, by default brings us to the thrust of this chapter—solving cross-browser responsive challenges.

Progressive enhancement versus graceful degradation

You're probably aware of the phrases "progressive enhancement" and "graceful degradation". These two concepts are methodologies for dealing with wide and varied browser support and spark fierce debate within the web community. Whilst initially they may seem inter-changeable terms, they are actually fundamentally opposed. Here's my take…

Graceful degradation means creating a site for modern browsers and then ensuring that certain older browsers are afforded a usable experience. Features degrade in older browsers and there is usually a cut-off point in which the oldest browsers aren't supported. There are also occasions where users are merely warned that there is a problem with their browser and workarounds are suggested (for example, "your browser is a joke—get a new one!")

Progressive enhancement is the reversal of graceful degradation. Progressive enhancement begins with markup that adheres to web standards, meaning it will be usable by all browsers (irrespective of technologies such as JavaScript and even CSS). The experience is then progressively enhanced for more capable browsers through CSS styling and eventually JavaScript (if required).

There are hundreds of articles discussing the merits and failures of each approach. For starters, I'd take a look at this piece on the Opera developer's site: `http://dev.opera.com/articles/view/graceful-degradation-progressive-enhancement/` and this excellent piece by Aaron Gustafson: `http://www.alistapart.com/articles/understandingprogressiveenhancement`.

Reality

Currently, progressive enhancement is largely considered to be the best practice way of developing a website. However, the cold hard truth is that whilst I fundamentally favor and build sites using the progressive enhancement methodology, there are plenty of instances where I am arguably doing things in a graceful degradation manner. How so?

The www.andthewinnerisnt.com site we have just built up uses HTML5 as its code base. Older browsers such as Internet Explorer versions 6, 7, and 8 (from this point on, also referred to as "old IE") were built and released before HTML5 (which you'll remember isn't a ratified standard despite its growing ubiquity) and so don't understand what <aside>, <section>, and <footer> elements are for. So, from a purist sense it could be argued I shouldn't be using HTML5 elements. By adding a piece of JavaScript to fix this basic functionality problem — is this really progressive enhancement?

Despite this, unless there is a compelling reason not to, I always opt to use HTML5 over HTML 4.01. The reality is that for the work I do on a week-in week-out basis, HTML5 offers more benefits than shortcomings. So, if using HTML5 (and I certainly recommend you do), give all devices the best shot at handling it natively by coding standards compliant HTML code (use the HTML5 validator at http://validator. nu/ or at http://validator.w3.org/ to eliminate any errors).

Regardless, there will inevitably be a point in which you choose (or are forced) to make some portion of the enhanced functionality afforded by modern browsers, possible in ailing versions of Internet Explorer. Maybe you want border-radius to work in old IE, for example. However, before you go there, I'm going to bend your ear just a little more...

Should you fix old versions of Internet Explorer?

At this point I'd like to re-iterate an earlier point: it's almost certainly possible to polyfill the majority of HTML5 and CSS3 features for older browsers but the resulting user experience will be heavily laden with JavaScript and potentially less usable than it would be without the polyfills. Needless to say, it's important to consider the performance implications of such a choice. Just because you can, doesn't mean you should!

Furthermore, even without polyfills (which we shall look at shortly), in my experience, adding, testing, and configuring IE specific CSS code to make IE6 and IE7 (and to a lesser extent IE8 and IE9) render pages so they look as similar as possible to a modern standards compliant browser takes at least as much time as visually enhancing a site for modern browsers — just far less enjoyable! Is that how you or your client want to spend the allocated development time?

Statistics (again)

Let's revisit some of the ground we covered in *Chapter 1, Getting Started with HTML5, CSS3, and Responsive Web Design*. Whilst conceding that statistics are always open to interpretation, we noted that from July 2010 to July 2011 global mobile browser usage (as measured by Global Stats at `http://gs.statcounter.com`) had risen (from 2.86 percent to 7.02 percent) whilst usage of Internet Explorer 7 had dropped (to 5.45 percent). For the last month of 2011, the stats are even more revealing: Internet Explorer 7 was just 4 percent with Internet Explorer 6 enjoying just 1.78 percent. Mobile browser usage meanwhile had increased to 8.04 percent.

An even more interesting fact is that for December 2011, a single modern browser, Google's Chrome (I'm including both, versions 15 and 16), accounted for 25.7 percent of global browser usage; almost the same amount accounted for by versions 6,7, and 8 of Internet Explorer (27.9 percent). Once you then factor the numbers for other modern browsers such as Safari (4.3 percent, excluding the iOS version) and all versions of Firefox (21.01 percent), and then the relevant mobile browsers, it's not difficult to appreciate that developing and enhancing the user experience for modern browsers, rather than patching up the holes in old ones makes more sense. At least to me!

The bottom line: usage of ailing versions of Internet Explorer (6, 7, and 8) is diminishing whilst usage of modern browsers (both desktop and mobile) is increasing.

Personal choice

Currently, my personal stance for new website builds is that I ensure tight visuals in the current version of Internet Explorer (v9 at the time of writing) and the nearest prior version (for example, IE8). Tweaking layout and style issues in older versions is then negotiable due to the additional time needed.

That doesn't mean I simply disregard any fundamental usability problems with versions such as IE7, I merely limit development time to ensure that basic layout and functionality works, and disregard minor alignment issues and visual enhancements that aren't supported within the browser such as background gradients, rounded corners, box-shadows, and so on. These things don't affect usability; for the most part they are merely progressive enhancements that I wouldn't expect (and nor should anyone else!) to see on aging browsers.

Testing sites across multiple browsers

Typically, standards compliant browsers, such as Chrome, Safari, and Firefox, render HTML5 and CSS3 based web pages pretty similarly. At present, the majority of smart phones (those based on Android and iOS), like their desktop Safari and Chrome counterparts, use WebKit as their base and also render pages as you would expect. However, the different versions of Internet Explorer are entirely different and there'll no doubt come a point where you'll need to check your design there too (unless it's your default browser in which case you have my sympathy). I usually use **IE Tester** (`http://www.my-debugbar.com/wiki/IETester/ HomePage`) — a free utility to run multiple versions of Internet Explorer on a single machine. However, there are plenty of alternatives and this feature on Smashing Magazine gives a good overview of some common choices:

`http://www.smashingmagazine.com/2011/08/07/a-dozen- cross-browser-testing-tools/`

To illustrate this approach, after looking at `http://www.andthewinnerisnt. com` in IE8, it's obvious we've got some fundamental work to do, merely making it functional. We're going to use a great JavaScript tool called Modernizr and a polyfill to patch things up for old IE. I'm not sure that IE deserves it after all the pain it causes but that's just the kind of guy I am. However, before we get to that, let's understand Modernizr a little more.

Modernizr—the frontend developer's Swiss army knife

The web community's ability to figure out the many and varied issues of cross browser compatibility and create solutions for mere mortals like myself never ceases to amaze and delight me. Modernizr was mentioned briefly in *Chapter 4, HTML5 for Responsive Designs* and again in the last chapter. To reiterate, Modernizr is an open source JavaScript library that feature tests a browser's capabilities. Fauk Ateş wrote the first version, and the project now also includes Alex Sexton and the incredibly talented Paul Irish as the lead developer. It's a tool of choice for a few companies you may have heard of — Twitter, Microsoft, and Google. I mention this not merely to blow smoke up the Modernizr team (although they certainly deserve it) but more to illustrate that this isn't merely *today's* great piece of JavaScript. Put bluntly, it's a tool that is worth understanding.

So what does it actually do? How does it enable us to both polyfill older browsers and progressively enhance the user experience for newer ones and how do we make it do what we need? Read on grasshopper...

In terms of actions, Modernizr does little, by default, other than add Remy Sharp's HTML5 shim (when selected) to enable structural HTML5 elements such as `<aside>` and `<section>` in non-HTML5 capable browsers such as IE 8 and lower versions. What it does is "feature test" the browser. Consequently, it knows whether said browser supports various features of HTML5 and CSS3. This then provides the means to take a different action depending upon that information. The rest is for us to implement. So, let's add Moderniz to our pages and make a start.

First, download Modernizr (`http://www.modernizr.com`).

Which version of Modernizr—development or production?

If you're interested in how it works, grab the development version of Modernizr as each option/test is documented. However, using the production option allows you to select only the tests that are relevant to the site or web application you are building, keeping the file nice and lean.

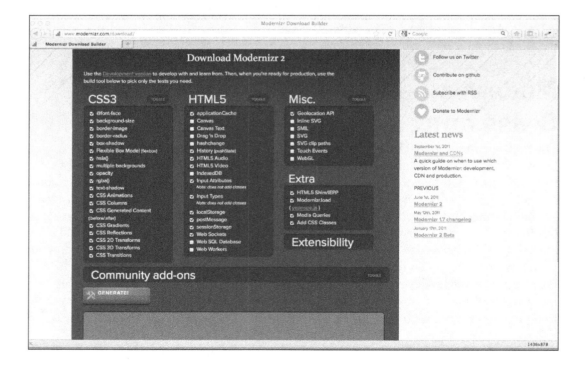

Now, save the file to a suitable location (as before I've used a `js` folder in the root). And then call the file in `<head>` of your page:

```
<head>
<meta charset=utf-8>
<meta name="viewport" content="width=device-width,initial-
scale=1.0,maximum-scale=1" />
<title>And the winner isn't…</title>
<link href="css/main.css" rel="stylesheet" />
<script src="js/modernizr.js"></script>
</head>
```

With Modernizr added, when viewing the source code of a page in Firebug or similar, it shows a variety of different classes added to the HTML tag. Here's an example from Firefox v9.01:

```
<html class=" js flexbox geolocation postmessage indexeddb history
websockets rgba hsla multiplebgs backgroundsize borderimage
borderradius boxshadow textshadow opacity cssanimations csscolumns
cssgradients no-cssreflections csstransforms no-csstransforms3d
csstransitions fontface generatedcontent video audio localstorage
sessionstorage applicationcache" lang="en">
```

This is great. It tells us, on a browser-by-browser basis, what features it has tested and which features the browser does or doesn't support (where there is no support for a feature, it prefixes the feature with `no-`). This lets us do two major things—fix styling issues on a feature-by-feature basis in our CSS files and also conditionally load additional CSS or JS files only when needed.

Fix styling issues with Modernizr

Our responsive *And the winner isn't…* site is presenting the perfect opportunity to fix a problem with Modernizr. Whilst the Quiz page (`http://www.andthewinerisnt.com/3Dquiz.html`) works fine in browsers (such as Safari and Chrome) that support 3D transforms it's just a simple hover effect in browsers that don't. Currently, regardless of whether a browser can render the 3D transforms or not, we have a note telling people: This page relies on 3D transforms. If the posters don't flip on hover, try viewing in Safari or Chrome.

But thanks to Modernizr's additional classes, we now have a means of only showing a relevant note if their browser *doesn't* have the 3D transform feature.

```
.note {
  display: none;
```

```
}
.no-csstransforms3d .note {
  display: block;
}
```

Breaking that down, first we set the CSS to not show the note by default:

```
.note {
  display: none;
}
```

This means browsers that have the CSS 3D Transform feature (Google Chrome 16 for example) won't see the note (see the following screenshot):

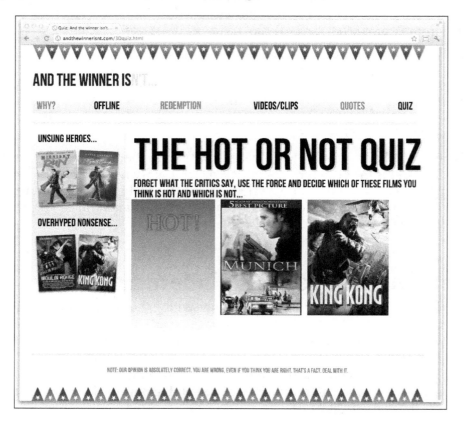

Then the second rule uses the additional class added by Modernizr to show the note for browsers that don't have the 3D transforms feature:

```
.no-csstransforms3d .note {
  display: block;
}
```

The following screenshot shows the same page in Firefox 9:

Modernizr allows us to stop thinking in terms of browsers and think in terms of features.

Modernizr adds HTML5 element support for old IE

As I've chosen a custom production version of Modernizr, that includes the HTML5 shim, refreshing the page in Internet Explorer 8 reveals a web page (as shown in the following screenshot) that looks a whole lot better than it did before:

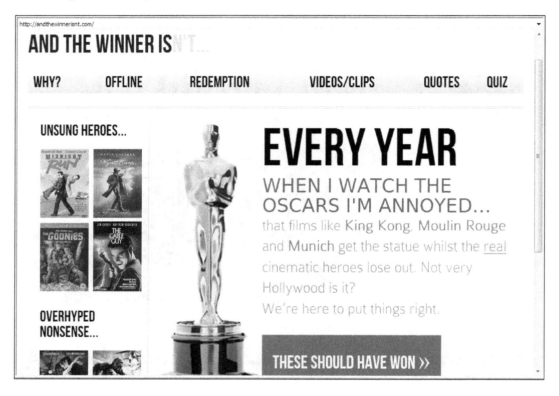

I didn't need to do anything more. Because Modernizr has enabled HTML5 structural elements in old IE many standard CSS styles are now understood and the page renders as it should.

For my money, that is perfectly usable. If you hadn't seen the same site in a modern browser you wouldn't necessarily know anything was different. However, due to IE8's lack of support for CSS3, we know there are some obvious visual shortcomings compared to a modern browser; there are no alternate colors in the navigation links (if needed we could easily fix this by adding an extra class to odd navigation links), no rounded corners on the button, no text or box shadows and perhaps more importantly, although our fluid grid flexes, a lack of CSS3 support means no media query support. No media queries—no significant layout changes at differing viewports in Internet Explorer 6, 7, or 8.

Although I don't consider this layout "broken" in any way, a tool such as Modernizr does give us the capability to add features that polyfill older browsers as we see fit. To illustrate, let's add media query min/max-width support so that our design responds to different viewports in Internet Explorer 6, 7, and 8.

Add min/max media query capability for Internet Explorer 6, 7, and 8

The polyfill that I generally use to add media query support to older versions of Internet Explorer only adds support for min/max-width media queries. There are more substantial media query polyfills that add a greater range of media query support but for a responsive design, **Respond.js** by Scott Jehl is simple to use, fast, and has always served me well.

Respond.js (`https://github.com/scottjehl/Respond`) can actually be used without Modernizr—just add it to the page in question, and as the author Scott Jehl himself says, "Crack open Internet Explorer and pump fists in delight".

So, before we integrate Respond.js with Modernizer, let's do just that. Drop Respond. js straight into our page (just add it after the Modernizr file we already added) and check it does what we want for IE. To do this, download the file, save it in a suitable location, and link to it in the `<head>` section:

```
<head>
<meta charset=utf-8>
<meta name="viewport" content="width=device-width,initial-
scale=1.0,maximum-scale=1" />
<title>And the winner isn't…</title>
<link href="css/main.css" rel="stylesheet" />
<script src="js/modernizr.js"></script>
<script src="js/respond.min.js"></script>
</head>
```

Now, once we load the page in Internet Explorer 8 and resize the browser window, we get our responsive design back (see the following screenshot):

Great, we've added a polyfill that sorts out min- and max-width media queries in Internet Explorer but here's the rub: this thing is now being loaded for every browser that loads the page—whether they need it or not. One solution would be to stick the script link in an IE conditional comment like the following:

```
<!--[if lte IE 8]>
        <script src="js/respond.min.js"/></script>
<![endif]-->
```

I'm sure you've come across conditional comments before. They are a simple way of loading CSS or JS files (or even content) that only the relevant version of Internet Explorer will use. All other browsers will see the code as a comment and ignore it.

In this example, our conditional comment says, "If you are *less than or equal* to (the lte part) Internet Explorer 8, (the IE 8 part) do this".

All about conditional comments

Conditional comments are falling out of favor compared with feature detection but if you'd like to know more, read all about them at the following URL:

`http://msdn.microsoft.com/en-us/library/`
`ms537512%28v=vs.85%29.aspx`

That will work fine. But do we really want to litter our markup with IE specific conditional comments? And what about polyfills for other browsers? This is where Modernizr steps up to the plate.

Conditional loading with Modernizr

A big pull of Modernizr when trying to keep websites and web applications as lean as possible is that it can load resources (both CSS and JS files) conditionally. So, rather than use a "scatter gun" approach and laden our pages with every polyfill a user *might* need (regardless of whether they actually need them or not), we only load the polyfills a user *actually* needs. This keeps our pages and load times as lean as they can be for each and every user.

So with Modernizr already added to the head of our pages, let's use it to conditionally load our Respond.js polyfill only if the browser in question doesn't natively understand CSS3 media queries (for example IE versions 6, 7, and 8).

Modernizr includes a JavaScript micro-library called **YepNope.js** (`http://yepnopejs.com/`). It uses a simple format:

```
Modernizr.load({
    test: Modernizr.mq('only all'),
    nope: 'js/respond.min.js'
});
```

First up is the call to the resource loading part of Modernizr:

```
Modernizr.load({
```

Within this is the test itself and a number of possible actions based on the result of that test. In this example, we have asked if the browser understands a media query:

```
test: Modernizr.mq('only all'),
```

If not, the resource should load our `respond.min.js` file:

```
nope: 'js/respond.min.js'
```

Here `only all` is the equivalent of "do you understand media queries?" Old IE will always fail the test, resulting in `nope` and therefore load the relevant resource. This enables `respond.min.js` to only be loaded when needed.

We could also opt to load additional files at the same time:

```
Modernizr.load({
    test: Modernizr.mq('only all'),
    nope: ['js/respond.min.js', 'css/extra.css']
});
```

This example uses an array to add the `respond.min.js` file and a CSS file called `extra.css`. You may opt to load CSS this way to maintain separate styles that are only needed in the presence or absence of certain features. It's worth remembering that it's also possible to load different resources based on different outcomes:

```
Modernizr.load({
    test: Modernizr.mq('only all'),
    yep: 'js/pass.js',
    nope: 'js/respond.min.js'['fail-polyfill.js', 'fail.css'],
    both: 'js/for-all.js'
});
```

Here, we load one file if the browser passes, another two (in the array) if it fails and a final file if it passes *or* fails.

The conditional loading code tests can be written in another separate JavaScript file. In this instance, I have called mine the `conditional.js` file and saved it in the `js` folder, alongside `modernizr.js` and `respond.min.js`. So, the `<head>` section now looks as follows:

```
<head>
<meta charset=utf-8>
<meta name="viewport" content="width=device-width,initial-
scale=1.0,maximum-scale=1" />
<title>And the winner isn't…</title>
<link href="css/main.css" rel="stylesheet" />
<script src="js/modernizr.js"></script>
<script src="js/conditional.js"></script>
</head>
```

Note that I've removed `respond.min.js` from the `head` as it's now loaded in conditionally as and when needed.

 More documentation on how to conditionally load resources with Modernizr can be found at `http://www.modernizr.com/docs/#load`

Get your polyfills here

Remember, there's a great repository (pun intended) of useful polyfills at the following Github location:

```
https://github.com/Modernizr/Modernizr/wiki/HTML5-
Cross-browser-Polyfills
```

Changing navigation links to a drop menu (conditionally)

A common issue with responsive designs is that if you have lots of navigation links on a page they can take up a sizeable portion of your screen real estate in smaller viewports.

For example, with only six page links, this is how any page currently loads for the *And the winner isn't...* website on a smaller viewport:

I'd like to swap those links out for a drop menu but only if a browser is below a certain viewport width. Now, you can roll your own piece of JavaScript to convert the menu items to a drop menu. The venerable Chris Coyier has documented how this can be achieved (`http://css-tricks.com/convert-menu-to-dropdown/`). Alternatively, there are a few pre-written scripts that do this for you. For brevity and ease, I have opted to use one such script. The following screenshot shows what the drop menu does to our navigation links on smaller viewports:

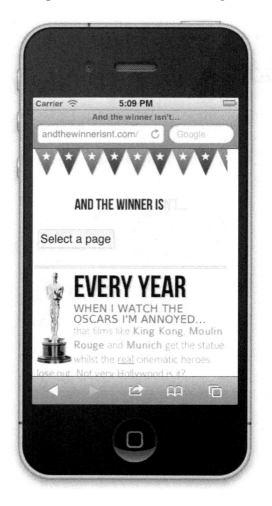

Clicking on the **Select a page** button brings up the navigation, as shown in the following screenshot:

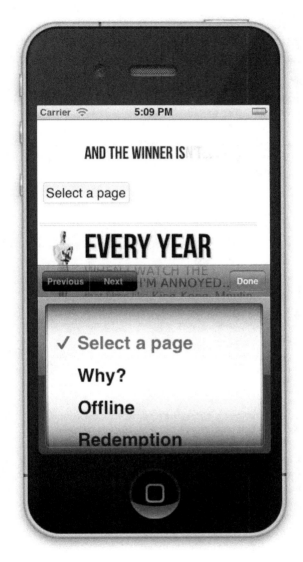

A perfect poster child for progressive enhancement—it isn't essential functionality but it gets more content "above the fold" for users with smaller viewports. So, let's get on and implement it. First off, download the Responsive Menu script (https:// github.com/mattkersley/Responsive-Menu). As before, save the relevant file (jquery.mobilemenu.js) to the js folder. There is just one thing we need to do first in the markup, and that's give our navigation links in each page an id:

```
<nav role="navigation">
  <ul id="mainNav">
    <li><a href="why.html">Why?</a></li>
    <li><a href="offline.html">Offline</a></li>
    <li><a href="redemption.html">Redemption</a></li>
    <li><a href="video.html">Videos/clips</a></li>
    <li><a href="quotes.html">Quotes</a></li>
    <li><a href="3Dquiz.html">Quiz</a></li>
  </ul>
</nav>
```

We could live without doing this but jQuery selectors work much faster with a specific id to latch onto.

Now, in the conditional.js file, we'll add the following code:

```
Modernizr.load([
  {
    test: Modernizr.mq('only all'),
    nope: 'js/respond.min.js'
  },
  {
    // load the menu convertor if max-width is 600px;
    test: Modernizr.mq('only screen and (max-width: 600px)'),
    yep : ['js/jquery-1.7.1.js', 'js/jquery.mobilemenu.js'],
    complete : function () {
      // Run this after everything in this group has downloaded
      // and executed, as well everything in all previous groups
      $(document).ready(function(){

          $('#mainNav').mobileMenu({
            switchWidth: 600,                 //width (in px to
switch at)
            topOptionText: 'Select a page',   //first option text
            indentString: '   ' //string for indenting
nested items
          });
      });


    }
  }
]);
```

After the prior conditional load that adds Respond.js for old IE, we've added another test:

```
test: Modernizr.mq('only screen and (max-width: 600px)'),
```

The previous test asks, does this viewport understand media queries and if it does, is the maximum width of the viewport 600px? If it does...

```
yep : ['js/jquery-1.7.1.js', 'js/jquery.mobilemenu.js'],
```

The previous line loads both the jQuery library and the Responsive Menu file:

```
complete : function () {
...more code...
```

The complete section effectively says, once any files are downloaded and executed, run the following:

```
$(document).ready(function(){

        $('#mainNav').mobileMenu({
            switchWidth: 600,                //width (in px to
switch at)
            topOptionText: 'Select a page',  //first option text
            indentString: '   ' //string for indenting
nested items
        });
});
```

These are the variables for the Responsive Menu script. Most importantly, the first option defines what viewport width I want the existing menu to be converted to a drop down (I've set it to 600px).

Again, using Modernizr to perform this task removes extraneous code for users that don't need it and allows progressive enhancement of the user experience for those that do.

For website designers, especially those unfamiliar with JavaScript, plunging into Modernizr for the first time can be daunting. There's certainly a lot to take in but hopefully this short primer will illustrate some obvious advantages that can be utilized in any future responsive project you might work on.

High resolution devices (the future)

Devices and their capabilities are changing all the time. Indeed, it isn't just different viewport sizes we must contend with. Already, we need to consider viewports that have higher resolution displays. The iPhone 4 was the first widely used device to implement a **high-resolution** display. Its screen is 960 by 640 pixel resolution at 326 pixels per inch, double the resolution of the prior version (iPhone 3GS) and double the pixel per inch density of laptops such as the 2011 15" MacBook Pro. Expect many more devices from tablets and laptops to desktop screens to follow suit. Thankfully, our responsive tools already provide us with the capabilities to support enhancements for these devices.

Let's suppose we wanted to load a higher resolution version of a site logo for users of high-resolution displays. It's a situation I encountered when performing a recent redesign of my own website at `http://www.benfrain.com`. Here is the markup for my logo area:

```
<div class="logo">
  <a href="http://benfrain.com/"></a>
</div>
```

And here is the CSS rule that loads the logo:

```
#container header[role="banner"] .logo a {
  background-image: url("../img/logo2.png");
  background-repeat: no-repeat;
  background-size: contain;
  display: block;
  height: 7em;
  margin-top: 10px;
}
```

Initially, the logo looked like the one shown in the following screenshot:

Perfectly functional but I wanted the logo as crisp as possible on higher resolution displays. So, I made two further versions of my logo (one for the default state and one for the hover state) at double the size of the existing logo and named them `logo2@x2.png` and `logo2Over@x2.png`. I then added the following media query in my CSS:

```
@media all and (-webkit-min-device-pixel-ratio : 1.5) {
  #container header[role="banner"] .logo a {
    background-image: url("../img/logo2@x2.png");

  }
```

```
    #container header[role="banner"] .logo a:hover {
      background-image: url("../img/logo2Over@x2.png");
    }
  }
}
```

The media query targets devices with a minimum device pixel ratio of 1.5. Therefore, high-resolution displays like those on the iPhone 4 and later come into this category and render the styles within. You'll notice this rule includes a `-webkit-` prefix. As ever, remember relevant prefixes for the devices you need to target.

And now, with high-resolution devices, the higher quality version of the logo is loaded instead, as shown in the following screenshot:

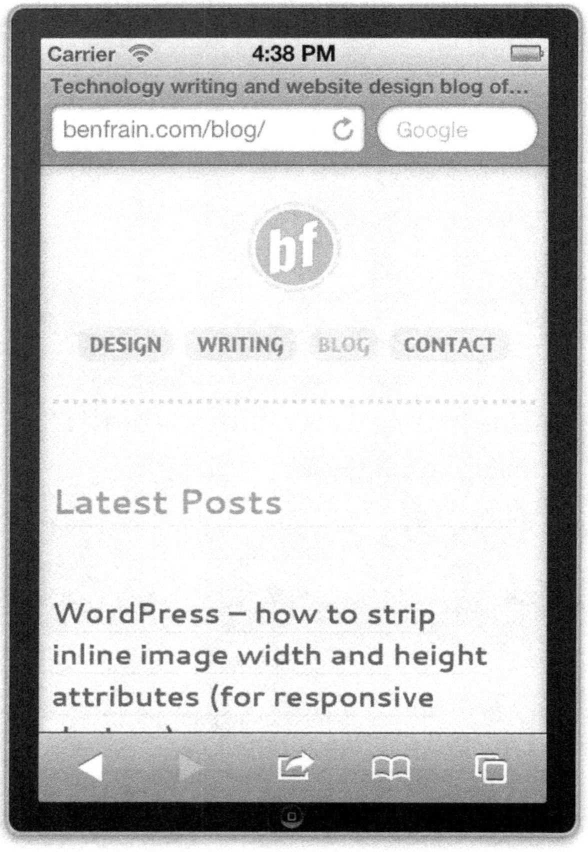

Admittedly, the difference is subtle. It's probably best to look at the differences in the flesh to appreciate the difference but the more detailed the image, the more likely it is to appear beautifully crisp on a high resolution display.

There are considerations to using this technique. Larger images equate to larger file sizes and longer download times so again, just because you can, doesn't mean you should.

Where supported, **Scalable Vector Graphics (SVG)** alleviate many of the image scaling issues that we currently face. As the name suggests, they are designed to produce images that can display crisply at whatever scale is needed. However, media queries and SVG don't help with inline photos for high resolution displays. You'll need to implement JavaScript based solutions in those instances.

Summary

In this chapter, we've considered the fundamental differences between progressive enhancement and graceful degradation. We've then used a polyfill to make old IE understand our media queries so that our design responds there too. Finally, we used Modernizr to conditionally load CSS and JavaScript files based upon any number of feature tests, thereby allowing us to serve up polyfills and additional or alternate styles only when a browser lacks the requisite features. Finally, we've taken a sneak peek at the technologies that are becoming commonplace in the immediate future and how we can use CSS3 to serve yet further enhancements for the devices that support them.

At this point, your humble author believes (and hopes) he has related all the techniques and tools you'll need to start building your next website or web app responsively.

It's my firm conviction that currently, responsive web designs built with HTML5 and CSS3 represent the best frontend development option for the vast majority of websites. With only a little modification to our existing workflows, practices, and techniques they enable us to provide fast, flexible, and maintainable websites that can look incredible regardless of the viewport used to visit them.

As mobile device usage continues to grow exponentially, and new devices that we never before contemplated enter the browsing fray, this methodology arguably provides the surest and most future proof means of building designs that will work on any device, on any viewport, and render as quickly as possible however those devices connect to the web.

Index

H

I

J

[PACKT]
PUBLISHING

Thank you for buying
Responsive Web Design with HTML5 and CSS3

About Packt Publishing

Packt, pronounced 'packed', published its first book "*Mastering phpMyAdmin for Effective MySQL Management*" in April 2004 and subsequently continued to specialize in publishing highly focused books on specific technologies and solutions.

Our books and publications share the experiences of your fellow IT professionals in adapting and customizing today's systems, applications, and frameworks. Our solution based books give you the knowledge and power to customize the software and technologies you're using to get the job done. Packt books are more specific and less general than the IT books you have seen in the past. Our unique business model allows us to bring you more focused information, giving you more of what you need to know, and less of what you don't.

Packt is a modern, yet unique publishing company, which focuses on producing quality, cutting-edge books for communities of developers, administrators, and newbies alike. For more information, please visit our website: www.packtpub.com.

Writing for Packt

We welcome all inquiries from people who are interested in authoring. Book proposals should be sent to author@packtpub.com. If your book idea is still at an early stage and you would like to discuss it first before writing a formal book proposal, contact us; one of our commissioning editors will get in touch with you.

We're not just looking for published authors; if you have strong technical skills but no writing experience, our experienced editors can help you develop a writing career, or simply get some additional reward for your expertise.

Dreamweaver CS5.5 Mobile and Web Development with HTML5, CSS3, and jQuery

ISBN: 978-1-84969-158-1   Paperback: 284 pages

Harness the cutting edge features of Dreamweaver for mobile and web development

1. Create web pages in Dreamweaver using the latest technology and approach

2. Add multimedia and interactivity to your websites

3. Optimize your websites for a wide range of platforms and build mobile apps with Dreamweaver

HTML5 Multimedia Development Cookbook

ISBN: 978-1-84969-104-8   Paperback: 288 pages

Recipes for practical, real-world HTML5 multimedia-driven development

1. Use HTML5 to enhance JavaScript functionality. Display videos dynamically and create movable ads using JQuery

2. Set up the canvas environment, process shapes dynamically and create interactive visualizations

3. Enhance accessibility by testing browser support, providing alternative site views and displaying alternate content for non supported browsers

Please check **www.PacktPub.com** for information on our titles

HTML5 Mobile Development Cookbook

ISBN:978-1-84969-196-3   Paperback: 254 pages

Over 60 recipes for building fast, responsive HTML5 mobile websites for iPhone 5, Android, Windows Phone, and Blackberry

1. Solve your cross platform development issues by implementing device and content adaptation recipes

2. Maximum action, minimum theory allowing you to dive straight into HTML5 mobile web development

3. Incorporate HTML5-rich media and geo-location into your mobile websites

jQuery UI 1.8: The User Interface Library for jQuery

ISBN: 978-1-84951-652-5   Paperback: 424 pages

Build highly interactive web applications with ready-to-use widgets from the jQuery User Interface Library

1. Packed with examples and clear explanations of how to easily design elegant and powerful front-end interfaces for your web applications

2. A section covering the widget factory including an in-depth example on how to build a custom jQuery UI widget

3. Updated code with significant changes and fixes to the previous edition

Please check **www.PacktPub.com** for information on our titles

CPSIA information can be obtained
at www.ICGtesting.com
Printed in the USA
LVHW101326140419
614130LV00010B/185/P

9 781849 693189